THE HYBRID AUTHORITY FORMULA

THE HYBRID
AUTHORITY
FORMULA

Delivering Transformational Learning at Scale

Matthew Mason

'As The Accountability Guy®, I have spent decades assisting high achievers to achieve real results – and Matthew Mason's *The Hybrid Authority Formula* is the blueprint everyone has been waiting for. This is more than just another book about digital delivery; it is a strategic blueprint for developing scalable learning experiences that change people's lives. What is the most important insight I have gained? Your job is more than just transferring knowledge. Your job is to effect meaningful change. This book provides exactly that: change by purpose, not by chance.'

Darren Finkelstein, The Accountability Guy®
www.tickthoseboxes.com.au

'Matthew Mason has written a truly thoughtful and practical book on how to deliver genuine transformation at scale. *The Hybrid Authority Formula* is what I'd call a "delivery philosophy". It feels like a sigh of relief for experts drowning in one-to-one delivery or disappointed by disengaged online courses. This book shows you how to deliver your work with more impact and more humanity. It's not just theory or rhetorical hype. It's smart, real, and long overdue. Every expert, coach, and thought leader should read this. Twice.'

Andrew Griffiths, International Bestselling Business Author
www.andrewgriffiths.com.au

'*The Hybrid Authority Formula* isn't just another book on online learning. It's a game plan for creating real impact at scale, without losing the personal touch. Matthew's insights are sharp, practical, and grounded in what actually works.'

Pratik 'Pat' Sharma, PLab Productions
www.plabproductions.com

'I found this book incredibly insightful and directly relatable as I build out the Institute of Trades Professionals hybrid business training. The strategies around structuring coaching for impact over volume and the focus on building a strong, connected community really hit home. Matthew's work has had a huge influence on how I approach program design and delivery. He's supported me greatly over time and continues to be an invaluable guide as we create transformational learning experiences for trade business owners.'

Matthew Jones, Institute of Trades Professionals
https://certification.instituteoftradesprofessionals.org

'*The Hybrid Authority Formula* is one of the most in-depth and valuable books I've ever read. Matthew does an incredible job of showing you how to build a business that not only provides freedom, but also brings real fulfillment. The insights on structuring a business you actually enjoy are absolutely mind-blowing. Matthew is a true expert in this space, and I can't recommend this book enough – it has the potential to truly change your life.'

Daniel Suckling, Subscription Kings
www.subscriptionkingz.com

'Matthew delivers some hard truths in this book about the problems with scaling online learning. *The Hybrid Authority Formula* delivers a practical and transformational design philosophy that you can implement today to get better results in your business.'

Jeremy Streten, Abundance Global
www.abundance.global

'After reading *The Hybrid Authority Formula*, I can hand on heart say that it was inspirational. It is so easy to read and follow with an excellent balance of not just how to effectively structure and deliver the subject matter, but I especially valued the emphasis included on how to meet the learners' needs and respect them as a human participant and not just as income.

'Every chapter kept delivering more "aha" moments, full of insights that resonated with the goals and challenges I have as a training provider. Throughout the first half of the book I felt so inspired and motivated by the possibilities of adopting the Hybrid Authority Formula, then soon realised that was only the launchpad for the second half of the book – which guides you through the practical systems and strategies to implement this powerful learning model. I am feeling so motivated to go and re-engineer all my current learning courses so they reflect this model.

'*The Hybrid Authority Formula* is an outstanding resource and essential reading for all coaches, facilitators, and training providers.'

Sarah Baum, Spirometry Training
https://learningportal.spirometrytraining.com.au

A catalogue entry for this book is available from the National Library of Australia.

ISBN: 978-1-923225-96-1

Book production and text design by Publish Central
Cover design by John Netro

The paper this book is printed on is certified as environmentally friendly.

Disclaimer: The material in this publication is of the nature of general comment
only, and does not represent professional advice. It is not intended to provide specific
guidance for particular circumstances and it should not be relied on as the basis for
any decision to take action or not take action on any matter which it covers. Readers
should obtain professional advice where appropriate, before making any such decision.
To the maximum extent permitted by law, the author and publisher disclaim all
responsibility and liability to any person, arising directly or indirectly from any person
taking or not taking action based on the information in this publication.

Contents

Preface

A new era of learning

The delivery dilemma

What happens when your impact no longer scales with your time?

If you're like most expert entrepreneurs – coaches, consultants, facilitators, or course creators – you probably built your business around your expertise. You spent years mastering your craft, growing your reputation, and delivering real results through direct, hands-on work with your clients. And somewhere along the way, you realized something deeply frustrating:

You can't keep doing it all live.

Whether it's one-on-one coaching sessions that overburden your calendar, virtual group calls that don't reach enough people, or digital courses that gather virtual dust, the tension is the same. You want to scale. You want to serve more people. But not at the cost of depth, transformation, or your own sanity.

That's exactly why the Hybrid Authority Formula was born.

This book – and the model it introduces – isn't about replacing the magic of live delivery or the freedom of digital courses. It's about creating something more powerful than what these are on their own. It's a flexible, high-impact delivery approach that combines your best thinking with scalable systems and human connection.

It's the difference between **delivering content** ... and **delivering transformation.**

After more than two decades working in learning design and supporting expert-led businesses, I've seen the same pattern play out over and over.

A consultant lands a high-ticket client but burns out trying to deliver every insight live.

A coach launches a course, only to see high drop-off rates and low engagement.

A facilitator builds a thriving business – until it stalls because they've maxed out their delivery hours.

They all hit the same wall: **the delivery dilemma.**

When you reach this point, you can either keep doing things manually and stay stuck at your current capacity, or you can try to scale with content and risk losing the human spark that made your work powerful in the first place.

But what if there was a better way?

What if you could package your IP, create digital content that lands, build a community that drives peer learning, foster collaboration, and still offer personal guidance ... all without burning out?

That's what the Hybrid Authority Formula offers: a proven structure for designing learning experiences that are transformational, scalable, and human.

The four key pillars of effective delivery

This is not a book about vague theory or educational trends. It's a **strategic playbook** for experts who want to build leveraged learning ecosystems without sacrificing results.

You'll learn how to:

- build your 'digital twin' – a **content** system that captures your expertise and delivers it with consistency and clarity
- create a **community** that fosters belonging, drives motivation, and increases learner success
- facilitate **collaboration** so learning becomes active, practical, and participatory
- deliver **coaching** that's scalable, personalized, and deeply impactful – without being constantly on call.

These four pillars – content, community, collaboration, and coaching – form the backbone of the Hybrid Authority Formula. Each one has its own section in this book, where we break down what it looks like in practice.

We also explore the **spectrum of learning experiences** – from inadequate and disengaging to transformative and lasting – and discuss how to design experiences that sit firmly on the far end of that spectrum: impactful, human-centered, and high-value.

Your job is to create meaningful change

If you've ever said ...

- 'I want to reach more people without lowering the quality of my program.'
- 'I'm exhausted by constant delivery and need to reclaim my time.'

- 'My content is solid, but my clients aren't getting the results I know are possible.'
- 'I want to stop trading time for money – but still be the go-to expert in my space.'

… this book is for *you.*

You don't have to choose between scale and depth. You don't have to be stuck in a position of fully digital or fully live delivery. There is a 'third path' – a hybrid approach that empowers you to grow your business while still transforming lives.

And it doesn't require reinventing everything from scratch.

In fact, if you have programs, content, coaching offers, or consulting IP, you're halfway there already. This book will help you repurpose, restructure, and reimagine your existing assets into a blended model that works for both you *and* your clients.

The engagement crisis

The last few years have reshaped how people learn. The explosion of online courses created an accessibility revolution – but also an engagement crisis. Completion rates are low. Communities feel empty. And more people than ever are asking: *'Is this working?'*

At the same time, live programs have become harder to scale. Zoom fatigue is real. People are more selective with their time. And coaches and consultants are burning out trying to overdeliver.

We're in the middle of a massive shift – and the experts who thrive won't be the ones with the fanciest tech or the biggest audiences.

They'll be the ones who master **hybrid delivery**. They'll know how to turn their knowledge into engaging content, facilitate collaboration, foster meaningful communities, and deliver coaching that gets results.

That's what it means to be a **Hybrid Authority** – not just an expert, but a transformational leader in your field with a delivery model to match.

At its core, this book isn't just about 'how' to deliver learning – it's about 'why.'

As a coach, consultant, or facilitator, your job isn't just to transfer knowledge. Your job is to create meaningful change. To help someone see a new perspective. Take new action. Step into a new version of themselves or their business.

That kind of transformation doesn't happen by accident; it's designed. And it's exactly what the Hybrid Authority Formula delivers.

So, as you move through the pages ahead, I invite you to think like a strategist. Reflect on your current programs. Look for leverage points. Consider not just what you teach, but how that teaching lands, sticks, and spreads.

Because the delivery model you build is part of your authority. It's what makes you scalable, referable, and transformational.

Let's get to work

We're about to walk through the four key pillars of the Hybrid Authority Formula. Each one will help you craft a program that scales your impact *without sacrificing depth*.

This isn't about theory. Everything in this book is implementation-ready.

So, whether you're starting from scratch or starting with a high-ticket coaching offer, a digital course that's lost steam, or a membership model that feels like a content treadmill ... this book will give you the clarity, structure, and tools to evolve. Because your expertise deserves to be delivered in a way that changes lives *and* frees yours.

Let's dive in.

Part I

THE PROBLEM AND THE POSSIBILITY

"

The quality of a learning experience lies
not in the quantity of information delivered,
but in how well it engages the learner
and changes their thinking.'

Stephen Brookfield[1]

"

---

1 Stephen Brookfield is a scholar of adult education and critical pedagogy, known for
   his work on reflective teaching and learner engagement. His research emphasizes that
   effective learning is measured not by content volume but by its impact on the learner's
   thinking and development.

Before you can design a better solution, you have to clearly name the problem.

The digital learning space is crowded – but not always effective. Many programs are overbuilt, under-engaging, or simply failing to deliver transformation. This part exposes the disconnect between what we create and what learners need.

You'll discover the engagement gap, the limits of content-first approaches, and the growing demand for hybrid learning that works.

This is where we define the problem, challenge the assumptions, and introduce a bold new path.

1

Why most digital courses are failing

Let's cut through the noise.

Online learning has exploded over the past decade, promising accessibility, scale, and profitability. Everywhere you look, experts are turning their knowledge into courses, memberships, and digital products. The promise is seductive: build it once and reap the passive income rewards. But here's the uncomfortable truth that nobody wants to talk about: most online programs aren't delivering the transformation they promise.

A few years ago, I worked with a leadership coach – we'll call her Dana – who had spent months recording the 'perfect' digital course. Twelve beautifully edited modules, bonus templates, even a custom-branded portal. The content and presentation were fantastic.

But three months post-launch, the data was clear: only 17% of her students had made it past module three. 'I feel like I built something nobody's using,' she told me. 'And worse – I don't know how to fix it.' She was facing what most expert entrepreneurs eventually discover: great content alone doesn't create transformation.

They might look great on the surface – slick landing pages, polished videos, and a branded portal – but under the hood, many of these programs are struggling. Completion rates are low. Engagement is minimal. Learners sign up with enthusiasm, only to disappear after completing just two or three modules. Coaches and consultants who thought they were building leverage find themselves burning out trying to keep clients on track, trying to generate enough sales, or quietly questioning whether they're making a difference.

This isn't a criticism. It's a reality check.

The myth of 'set and forget'

You're not alone if you've launched a course and watched it collect digital dust. Or if you've delivered a group program where half the participants never showed up. The gap between what we teach and what lands is growing wider in the digital age – not because we lack expertise, but because we're relying on delivery methods that don't reflect how people truly learn, apply, and transform.

Self-paced courses

Let's start with self-paced courses. They're often positioned as the holy grail of scalability. Record your content, set up your automation, and sell it while you sleep. And yes, from a delivery standpoint, it's efficient. Learners can consume content anytime, anywhere.

But here's the catch: flexibility without structure often leads to abandonment.

In theory, learners love the idea of controlling the pace. In practice, life gets in the way. Without accountability, human connection, or a reason to keep showing up, that 'on-demand freedom' becomes a permission slip to procrastinate. Most people don't lack access to information – they lack structured support to act on it. That's the critical difference.

Sam, a solo business owner, bought a self-paced pricing course with good intentions. 'I watched the first video on a Sunday night and felt inspired,' he told me. 'But then Monday hit. I told myself I'd get back to it. I never did.' He didn't fail because he wasn't smart or committed. He just didn't have a system strong enough to carry him forward.

Membership programs

Membership programs promise continuity and community, but they often suffer from another hidden pitfall: churn. You can fill a membership once, but keeping people engaged month after month requires a level of strategic design most creators underestimate. Without clear outcomes or progression pathways, members float aimlessly. The result? They cancel quietly, leaving you with a leaky revenue bucket. Worse, they often leave feeling that they've failed, when in fact the model failed them.

Virtual group coaching

Virtual group coaching has gained traction as a middle ground – a blend of live interaction with the leverage of group delivery. But when all the value is locked inside weekly Zoom calls, you're still tied to your calendar. If every insight depends on being in the room live, your program can't scale beyond your availability. Worse, it leaves those who can't attend live in a passive observer role, consuming replays instead of participating in real time.

One-to-one coaching

And then there's traditional one-to-one coaching. Deeply transformative? Yes. High impact? Absolutely. But it's also the most time-bound, energy-intensive model of all. You're paid well, but you're still trading hours for outcomes. The moment you stop, the revenue stops too. The bottleneck isn't your content – it's your calendar.

The real reasons learners drop off

At the core of all these models is a common oversight: they prioritize *delivery efficiency* over *learning effectiveness*. It's not that the formats are wrong – it's that they're incomplete.

The missing pieces: no structure or support

When learners disengage, it's rarely because the content isn't good. More often, it's because the learning experience doesn't support them as whole humans navigating change. People don't just need information. They need activation. They need context. They need a reason to care – and a path to follow.

They need motivation and momentum. They need to feel part of something. They need small wins to keep going and meaningful touchpoints to ask, 'Am I on the right track?' They need to be seen. Heard. Encouraged.

This is where traditional online models fall short. They focus on information transfer, not transformation. And in the real world, transformation requires traction – the kind that happens through interaction, reflection, feedback, and application. That's why we see learners ghosting their own goals. Not because they don't care, but because the program isn't strong enough to hold their attention, energy, and effort through the inevitable dips of learning something new.

Most online programs leave too much to chance. They assume the learner will take initiative, stay engaged, and push through resistance – without the kind of scaffolding essential in any high-quality learning environment.

That scaffolding needs to be built in from the beginning – not bolted on as an afterthought. It's not enough to drop a workbook in a module and call it support. It's not enough to have a private Facebook group that no one uses. These surface-level 'interactions' aren't enough to anchor someone in the learning process. Learners need real anchors – rhythms, routines, rituals.

They need feedback loops and check-ins. They need built-in ways to reflect and apply. They need space to connect, ask questions, and share progress.

But most creators aren't failing because they don't care. They're failing because they're modeling their programs on digital learning myths – not on what works.

The engagement gap: the fatal flaw of most digital learning

There's a gap that exists between what we create and what learners experience. We think we've built something valuable because we poured our knowledge into a series of videos or a 12-week plan. But what matters isn't just what we deliver – it's how it's received.

When a program lacks interactivity, learners become passive. When there's no built-in feedback, learners become uncertain. When there's no sense of community, learners feel isolated.

And when learners feel passive, uncertain, and isolated? They disengage. Quietly. Politely. Completely.

And that disengagement is the fatal flaw of most digital learning.

Without engagement, there is no transformation. Without transformation, there is no lasting value. And without value, your reputation, referrals, and revenue all begin to plateau or decline.

Content creators must stop mistaking information for transformation. The job isn't simply to deliver content – it's to design learning that sticks.

That requires asking tougher questions: how does this piece of content help the learner take the next step? In what ways does it make them feel seen, supported, and challenged? And how is progress being measured?

These questions are the foundation of effective program design. They turn learning from a transaction into a transformation.

What the best programs do differently

The best learning experiences don't just deliver content – they engineer outcomes. They are intentionally designed to guide, support, and challenge learners every step of the way.

Jalen had a solid course, but his students weren't finishing – or succeeding. Together, we redesigned it using the hybrid model: we built in small-group sprints, pre-call prep rituals, and micro-coaching checkpoints. Within two months, his completion rate more than doubled, and one learner said, 'This is the first time I've actually followed through.' Jalen didn't add more content – he changed the experience.

The best programs combine structured, self-paced content with strategic opportunities for live connection. They build community not as an afterthought, but as an essential layer of support. They integrate coaching and collaboration to make learning active, not passive.

They foster psychological safety and make reflection a habit. They focus on implementation, not just absorption. And they include accountability mechanisms, regular check-ins, and clear milestones.

These programs recognize that scalable doesn't have to mean soulless. That systems can still be human. That growth can still be grounded in genuine support. And the people behind them understand something that most experts miss: it's not about creating more content. It's about creating the conditions for change.

The best programs are built from the learner's perspective. They understand that transformation is a process, not a purchase. And they meet learners where they are – while leading them forward with purpose and clarity.

They leverage a blend of content, coaching, collaboration, and community in a way that feels seamless. They anticipate the learner's questions before they arise. They don't just inform – they empower.

This kind of experience doesn't happen by accident. It happens by design. And it's exactly what the Hybrid Authority Formula empowers you to do.

A new standard: the hybrid solution

Content creators need a new model. One that maximizes the convenience of digital delivery but doesn't sacrifice the depth of human connection. One that empowers learners with flexibility and accountability. One that recognizes that the path to mastery isn't linear, and that learners need scaffolding, not just content.

This is where the Hybrid Authority Formula comes in.

THE HYBRID AUTHORITY FORMULA

SELF-GUIDED

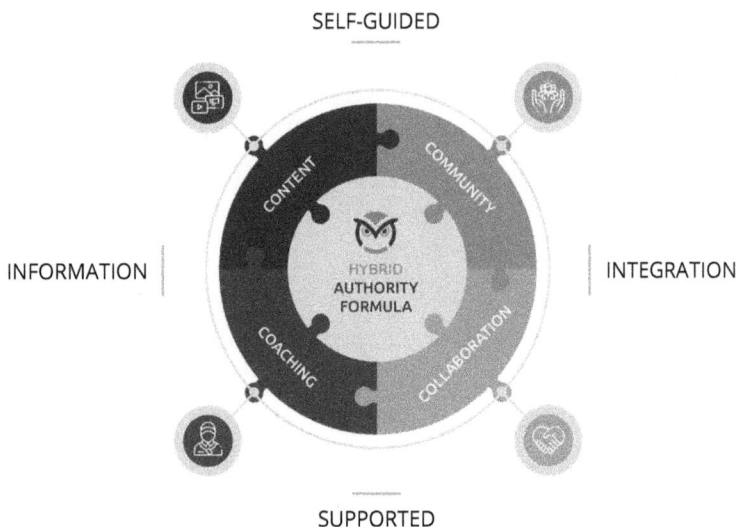

INFORMATION

INTEGRATION

CONTENT

COMMUNITY

HYBRID AUTHORITY FORMULA

COACHING

COLLABORATION

SUPPORTED

It's not a tactic or a tech stack. It's a framework for designing learning that changes people. A structure for delivering your expertise in a way that is both scalable and deeply supportive.

Hybrid learning doesn't mean splitting the difference. It means designing for the whole learner: their head, their heart, and their habits. It means blending the best of self-paced assets, community engagement, group collaboration, and personalized coaching into one cohesive experience.

And when you do that? You create something magnetic. You create something that not only delivers value, but keeps delivering it – through higher completion rates, better results, stronger testimonials, and more referrals.

You shift from being an expert with content to an authority with impact.

The Hybrid Authority Formula isn't just about delivery. It's about authority. In a crowded market of content creators, those who engineer transformation are the ones who lead.

So, if you're ready to leave behind the burnout of live-only delivery, the disappointment of disengaged learners, and the pressure to constantly 'do more' just to keep your business afloat – you're in the right place. This book is your blueprint for building learning experiences that scale your impact, elevate your authority, and set a new standard for what expert-led learning can be.

Let's reimagine what online learning should feel like – for you and for those you serve.

Because it's not just about building a better course. It's about building a better future – for your learners, your business, and your mission.

And it starts right here.

2

Why not all learning works the same

The spectrum of learning experiences

If you want to deliver transformation – not just information –
you must understand this: **not all learning experiences are
the same**. What you create, how you deliver it, and the outcomes it produces all depend on the learning experience you've
designed. And the truth is, most experts designing programs
today don't realize that there's more than one kind. They just
assume 'content = course' and stop there.

I want to introduce a critical truth: there are fundamentally
different types of learning experiences, and only one of them
consistently leads to scalable transformation.

I call this the 'spectrum of learning experiences.'

This spectrum isn't about *you*. It's not about your level as a
coach or creator. It's not about what stage your business is in
or how big your audience is. It's about the learning experience
you design. That experience – on its own – lands somewhere
on this spectrum.

Where a learning experience sits on this spectrum determines how well it engages, supports, and empowers the learner.

There are four types of learning experiences on the spectrum:

- inadequate
- informational
- interactive
- impactful.

THE SPECTRUM OF LEARNING EXPERIENCES

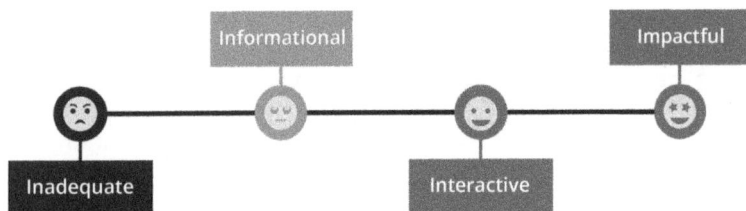

The learning experience you have created will confuse, inform, engage, or transform. Only one type – **impactful** – delivers the kind of authority, outcomes, and scalability the **Hybrid Authority Formula** is designed for.

Let's take a look at each category, to build awareness of what's possible – and what's worth leaving behind.

Inadequate learning experiences

This is the bottom end of the spectrum – not because of judgment or ego, but because of outcomes. **An inadequate learning experience is one that actively undermines the learner's ability to succeed.** It might be built with the best of intentions, but the result is confusion, frustration, and disengagement.

Such learning experiences are often thrown together without a cohesive structure, without a clear path forward, and without any meaningful support. They might contain valuable information, but it's scattered. They might offer lots of content, but there's no narrative thread to guide the learner. Navigation is confusing. Expectations are fuzzy. And the learner, often, is left frustrated, discouraged, or worse, convinced that the problem lies with them.

One creator I spoke with built a mini-course in a weekend using an AI prompt stack. On paper, it checked all the boxes: intro video, module structure, workbook. But feedback from learners was brutal. 'I didn't even know where to start,' one said. 'There was no momentum – just modules.'

The course wasn't just unhelpful. It left people doubting themselves. That's the true cost of an inadequate experience.

This is happening more than ever. With the rise of AI-generated courses flooding the market – quick builds promising quick wins – we're seeing a wave of programs that are technically complete but pedagogically broken. These experiences look finished on the surface, but the actual design lacks the depth, direction, and support required to create meaningful learning. They're built quickly, not thoughtfully. And learners feel that.

Even seasoned experts sometimes fall into this trap. They assume that because they've shared valuable content, they've delivered a valuable experience. But content on its own isn't enough. A library of lessons without a learning arc isn't an experience – it's a collection. And collections don't teach. They overwhelm.

This kind of experience erodes trust. It makes learners less likely to invest again, less likely to refer others, and less likely to implement what they were so excited about at the start.

Even if the intention was good – even if the creator knows their stuff – an inadequate learning experience is broken by design. Not because it's too short or too long. Not because of pricing. But because it doesn't lead the learner forward in a purposeful, supported way.

That's why this category sits at the bottom end of the spectrum. It doesn't support change. It sabotages it.

Informational learning experiences

This is where most digital courses land. The program is clean. Structured. Content-rich. The videos are clearly labelled. The interface is intuitive. Modules unfold in a logical order. And from the outside, it all appears to be working well.

But beneath that polish, something critical is missing.

Informational learning experiences rely almost entirely on the transmission of knowledge. The focus is on delivering content – usually through pre-recorded lessons or written content, accompanied by PDFs, checklists, or downloadable workbooks. The learner is expected to consume, comprehend, and implement. But that final piece – implementation – is where these experiences consistently fall short.

Learners may watch or read. They may absorb. They may even take notes. But they're still alone. There's no mechanism for reflection, no structured space for interaction, and no opportunity for guided application. There's no traction, no feedback, and no facilitation. And when questions arise – as they always do – there's nowhere to turn. The learner is left to navigate uncertainty on their own.

These experiences often deliver the 'what' and the 'why' very well. But they rarely deliver the 'how' – at least not in a way that sticks. And without support, even clarity can become a burden.

It creates a false sense of progress: the learner feels informed, but they're not truly equipped to change anything.

That's the trap of informational learning: it creates the illusion of momentum without the structure to sustain it.

These programs may look successful. They often sell well. They may receive surface-level praise: 'so much value,' 'really insightful.' But deeper transformation is rare. Learners may appreciate the material, but they don't act. They don't follow through. They don't *change*.

When real life kicks in – when time runs short or doubt sets in – informational learning is easily abandoned. Not because the content is bad, but because the experience lacks the scaffolding to keep learners in motion.

I once bought a course that promised to teach business systems in depth. What I got was five hours of video content split across just four giant videos – each more than an hour long, with no way to mark progress or resume where I left off. Even worse, the creator constantly veered off track with rambling personal stories that had little relevance to the core message. It wasn't that there was no information – there was plenty. But it was up to me to sift through it, extract the key points, and figure out what to do next. There was no structure, no interactivity, no support – just raw content. I didn't finish, not because I didn't care, but because the learning experience made it hard to care.

This is also the point where many well-meaning creators mistakenly assume that what's needed is simply 'more engagement.' So, they add more videos. They include more checklists. Maybe even a comment thread. But without intentional structure, those additions don't change the nature of the experience – they just dress it up.

People don't change because they've consumed content. They change when they're supported in applying it.

Informational learning is passive. Even the best content, when isolated, becomes inert. No matter how polished the portal or how thorough the resources, an experience that ends at understanding cannot lead to transformation.

That's why this category sits where it does on the spectrum: above chaos, but still a long way from change.

Interactive learning experiences

This is where learning starts to feel more alive. These experiences still rely on solid content, but now they introduce elements that invite the learner to engage. There might be group calls, live sessions, online forums, feedback loops, or collaborative projects.

Learners are no longer just watching – they're *participating*. The experience creates a sense of connection. Learners ask questions. They share wins. They interact with others on the same journey. And so they stay longer, retain more, and often feel more committed. The program starts to feel like a shared experience, not just a solo activity.

This engagement boosts motivation. When people feel seen, heard, and included, they're more likely to show up and stay involved. They're not just clicking through modules. They're contributing. They're reflecting. They're interacting with content, the coach, and their peers.

But there's a trap here – and it's easy to miss: interaction is not the same as transformation.

Many programs in this category feel dynamic but still fail to drive meaningful outcomes. They're active, but not always effective. There's energy in the room, but not necessarily clarity in the path. Learners might be present, vocal, even enthusiastic – but still unsure what to do next. Or worse, they take action that doesn't move them forward.

A leadership coach I worked with ran a powerful group experience, with weekly live Zoom sessions, real-time discussions, journaling prompts, and open Q&As. People showed up, shared openly, and left feeling seen. But a few months in, she noticed a pattern: her clients loved the calls, but few were applying the insights in their actual business. 'They kept having breakthroughs,' she said, 'but nothing changed between calls.' The interaction created emotional resonance – but without structured actions or integration, the transformation stalled.

The problem is the absence of intentional integration. Interaction for the sake of it doesn't create change. A group call with no structure is just another meeting. A Facebook group with no facilitation becomes a distraction. A prompt to 'engage' without feedback or follow-through is just noise. Without purposeful design, these interactions become disconnected from the outcomes they're supposed to support.

That's why this category is deceptive. It feels like progress is being made – both for the learner and the creator. Everyone's busy. There's activity. But activity alone isn't impact. And when learners eventually stall or plateau, there's no clear system in place to get them moving again.

This is the most dangerous kind of stuck: the kind that 'feels almost right.'

But 'almost right' doesn't scale. And it doesn't build authority.

An interactive learning experience is certainly better than an informational or inadequate one. It adds momentum. It creates community. It makes learning feel less lonely. But without a design that ties interaction directly to implementation, the experience will hit a ceiling. It's more engaging, yes – but still incomplete.

And incomplete experiences don't change lives. They just delay the drop-off.

This is why you don't stop here. The goal isn't just to create engagement. It's to create transformation. And for that, you need something stronger – something that blends the best of content, community, collaboration, and coaching into one intentional, outcome-driven journey.

And that's where the Hybrid Authority Formula begins to shine.

Impactful learning experiences

Impactful learning experiences are where real transformation happens – not occasionally, but consistently. These experiences aren't just better – they're fundamentally different. They're built from the ground up to support meaningful, measurable, and lasting change.

Impactful learning experiences are not defined by content volume, production quality, or the number of modules. They're defined by how deliberately every element of the experience is designed to help the learner progress. From the very beginning, every component is reverse engineered from the transformation the learner is meant to achieve. Nothing is accidental. Everything is aligned.

This is where hybrid learning lives.

The four pillars of the Hybrid Authority Formula – content, community, collaboration, and coaching – combine to create impactful learning experiences. And here's the key: none of those elements are optional. They work in synergy, each one amplifying the others to build a cohesive, supportive, and high-impact journey.

Content in an impactful learning program is not just well-organized – it's purposeful and actionable. It guides, it instructs, and it creates clarity at every step. But content alone is never the endpoint – it's the foundation. Around that foundation, community provides belonging and shared momentum. Collaboration gives learners the space to think, co-create, reflect, and implement. And coaching ensures they never have to navigate confusion alone. These elements aren't add-ons. They're integrated into the learning architecture.

Learners aren't just told what to do, they're supported in doing it. They're not left guessing or drifting. They're guided, challenged, and encouraged. They have access to feedback, they see examples of progress, and they know where to turn when something isn't working. Most importantly, they feel seen. And that emotional safety accelerates their learning far more than any single lesson ever could.

One of my business coaching clients works with tradespeople, who are practical, time-poor, and not particularly keen on 'traditional learning.' I helped him redesign his program using the hybrid model. Learners could access focused content in their own time, but the real shift came through structured collaboration: small group discussions, live coaching calls, and a simple weekly planning ritual that helped them apply what they learned immediately.

What surprised him most was the feedback after he made these changes. These weren't the kind of people who typically raved about programs, but they did. They said things like, 'This actually fits my life,' and 'I'm finally doing things differently at work.' The program didn't just generate strong results for them – it created visible improvements in the businesses they worked in. That's what real impact looks like.

This sets impactful learning apart. It's not just about transferring knowledge. It's about changing behavior. Empowering action. Delivering results. And doing it in a way that is scalable, sustainable, and deeply human.

These are the experiences that create the kind of outcomes people talk about, without being asked. They lead to unsolicited testimonials, organic referrals, and word-of-mouth momentum. They turn learners into loyal fans, clients into case studies, and programs into category leaders.

They don't just scale. They elevate.

This is the only kind of experience worth building if your goal is to deliver transformation at scale – and become a true authority in your field.

Because impact is not the result of content alone. It's the result of intentional, hybrid design. And that's exactly what the rest of this book will help you build.

So why does this matter?

You're not just building a program. You're building a learning experience. And the kind of experience you build determines everything else: how well your learners succeed, how much they value the work, how long they stay, and how far your message spreads.

The Spectrum of Learning Experiences is to show you what's possible – and if you're serious about delivering transformation, only one category counts.

Inadequate won't scale. Informational won't stick. Interactive won't sustain.

Only impactful hybrid experiences move the needle – for your learners, and for your legacy.

And now that you know the difference, there's no going back.

3

The hybrid shift: a framework for scalable transformation

The Hybrid Authority Formula isn't a buzzword or a gimmick. It's a strategic redesign of how expert entrepreneurs – coaches, consultants, and course creators – can deliver deeper transformation while building a more scalable, sustainable business.

Because the way most experts are currently delivering content simply isn't built to last.

Maybe you're stuck in an endless cycle of Zoom calls, trying to keep clients engaged. Maybe you've poured your knowledge into an evergreen course – only to find that completion rates are low, and impact feels limited. Or maybe you're doing life-changing work one-on-one, but every breakthrough depends on your direct involvement.

What you're bumping up against is the ceiling of traditional delivery models. Content without connection. Coaching without capacity. Community without clarity. It's not that your work isn't powerful – it's that the way it's delivered is exhausting you, limiting your income, and not reaching the people who need it most.

This isn't about doing more. It's about doing better. It's about blending the best of digital convenience with the power of human connection – designing experiences that don't just inform but *transform*.

The Hybrid Authority Formula is your pathway to more time, more income, and more influence. It's not just a method for scaling your business – it's a system for amplifying your authority and delivering real, lasting results at scale.

Before we break down what it looks like, let's clarify what it is – and what it *isn't*.

What the Hybrid Authority Formula is – and isn't

The Hybrid Authority Formula isn't just a new delivery model – it's a complete design philosophy. It's how you architect learning experiences that move beyond knowledge transfer and into the realm of deep, lasting transformation.

At its core, this formula combines four essential components – content, community, collaboration, and coaching – into a single, intentionally designed ecosystem. Not as a bolt-on. Not as 'nice to haves.' And definitely not as random add-ons scattered across different tools. The four pillars work in concert, creating a seamless journey that honors both the power of digital leverage and the irreplaceable value of human connection.

THE HYBRID AUTHORITY FORMULA ECOSYSTEM

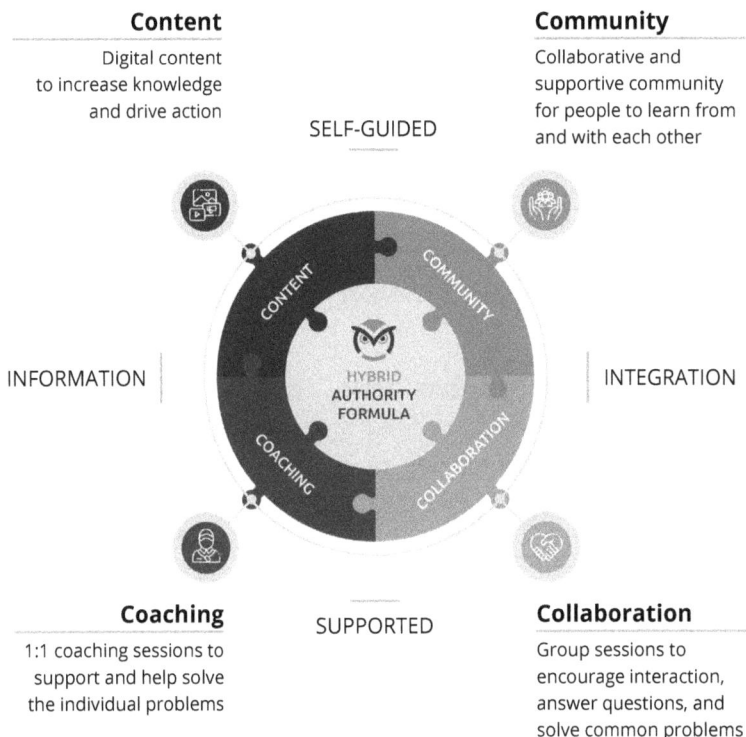

Content

Digital content to increase knowledge and drive action

Community

Collaborative and supportive community for people to learn from and with each other

SELF-GUIDED

INFORMATION

INTEGRATION

Coaching

1:1 coaching sessions to support and help solve the individual problems

SUPPORTED

Collaboration

Group sessions to encourage interaction, answer questions, and solve common problems

The Hybrid Authority Formula is not just a course with a Facebook group. It's not group coaching with some videos tacked on. It's not slapping a Zoom call on your calendar each week and calling your program 'hybrid.' And it's certainly not about doing more just to appear 'high touch.'

In fact, it's the opposite. The Hybrid Authority Formula is the antidote to hustle-heavy delivery. It offers a smarter, more sustainable way to scale without sacrificing depth. Where most self-paced courses fall flat because they leave learners isolated and most group coaching relies too heavily on the facilitator to carry the momentum, this model distributes the weight across a well-designed experience that invites autonomy and accountability.

It also moves you out of the trading-time-for-money trap. One-to-one consulting might feel meaningful, but it places a hard limit on your income and reach. And high-production online courses without human support might look scalable, but they rarely lead to the kind of transformation your clients truly want.

The magic of the Hybrid Authority Formula is in its balance. It respects your boundaries. It values your clients' transformation. And it builds a bridge between scale and service – a delivery model that works with your business goals, not against them.

Once you see how this formula fits together, you'll never look at learning design the same way again.

How hybrid learning boosts authority, impact, and scalability

Let's now examine how hybrid learning delivers authority, impact, and scalability, without compromising one for the others. This is how you grow your business without burning yourself out. This is how you expand your reach without sacrificing the depth of your work.

Authority

Your authority grows when your delivery moves beyond just real-time advice. When it becomes a structured system that clients can see, trust, and follow. By codifying your knowledge into frameworks and delivering it through a consistent journey, you're no longer just a helpful coach – you become a strategic architect who has built something solid, proven, and replicable. That shift elevates your brand and positions your intellectual property as a signature methodology, not just valuable content.

Impact

Your impact increases because the Hybrid Authority Formula addresses all three ingredients of real transformation:

- access
- accountability
- application.

Learners progress through an intentionally designed journey where they consume, connect, collaborate, and receive coaching. That kind of multi-layered experience doesn't just deliver knowledge – it drives change. It shifts behaviors, not just beliefs. And it embeds transformation in ways that stick.

Scalability

When your program is built around leveraged content, structured support, and peer-driven momentum, you're no longer the bottleneck. You can serve more clients more effectively, without being in every conversation, on every call, or solving every problem yourself. You move from over-burdened facilitator to empowered designer of results.

The four pillars behind the Hybrid Authority Formula

So, what makes this model work in practice? Let's take a closer look at the four pillars that provide the strength of the Hybrid Authority Formula.

Pillar one: content – building your digital twin

Think of your content as your 'digital twin' – the part of you that can teach, guide, and inspire without being in the room. Not just a timesaver, but a *presence multiplier*. With strategically designed digital assets, you can be everywhere your clients need you – without being *everywhere*.

Inside the Hybrid Authority Formula, content forms the foundation. But not all content is created equal. We're not talking about dumping hours of footage into a portal or cramming every detail into one long video. We're talking about clear, intentionally sequenced digital assets – short videos, visual models, bite-sized learning content, guided workbooks, and actionable templates – that build clarity, create momentum, and prepare learners for deeper application.

And the real power? It's in the flexibility your content provides to your clients. They can engage with it on their schedule, not yours. Whether during a quiet evening, a weekend sprint, or in between client calls, the learning is always ready. They're not stuck waiting for the next live call or rushing to keep up with a cohort timeline.

More than that, your well-structured program gives them freedom of *pace*. In a typical live setting, everyone moves at the speed of the middle. Fast learners get bored. Deep thinkers get left behind. But when content is self-paced and thoughtfully designed, each learner becomes the driver of their journey. They can pause, replay, skip ahead, or circle back as needed. No one's held back. No one's left behind.

And when learners arrive at group sessions or coaching calls having already engaged with your material? That's when the real work begins. They come with insights, not just questions.

They're ready to apply, not just absorb. Content doesn't replace you – it empowers everything else around you.

This is the shift: from content as a container for knowledge to content as the catalyst for transformation.

Pillar two: community – learning together, not alone

Despite the rise of on-demand everything, human beings don't thrive in isolation. We're wired for connection. And when it comes to learning, we grow best through interaction: watching others, reflecting out loud, asking messy questions, celebrating wins, and supporting each other through the hard parts.

That's not just intuition – it's science. Albert Bandura's Social Learning Theory tells us we don't learn only by doing, but by observing and modeling others – especially those we relate to or admire.[2] In other words, we learn better in a community.

That's why community isn't just a 'nice to have' in your program. It's an essential design element. It's where your learners make sense of your content. Where they test ideas in real life. Where they feel seen, supported, and accountable. It transforms a solo experience into a shared journey.

This might take the form of a curated peer group, a lively online space, or structured cohort threads. It doesn't have to be massive – it just must be intentional. Because when your clients see others wrestling with the same challenges, applying the same tools, and celebrating similar wins, they don't just learn more – they *believe* more. In the material. In the process. In themselves.

---

2   Albert Bandura is a Canadian–American psychologist and Professor of Social Science in Psychology at Stanford University.

And for you? Community becomes an insight engine. It's where you hear what's landing and what's being lost. It's where new ideas emerge, and where your next offer may take shape. Your role shifts from just teaching content to facilitating an ecosystem of engagement.

When you design with community in mind, you don't just create belonging – you create momentum. And that's what makes your program magnetic.

Pillar three: collaboration – from knowing to doing

Most learning stalls in the space between 'I understand' and 'I've implemented.' Collaboration is how you maintain the momentum.

Here's the shift: it's not enough for learners to *know* what to do. They need structured opportunities to *do* it – and do it together. Collaboration takes learning from the theoretical to the practical. It's the practice ground where learners build capability, confidence, and connection.

In the Hybrid Authority Formula, collaboration shows up through live group sessions, implementation sprints, breakout workshops, and guided peer feedback. The structure may vary, but the goal remains the same: get learners actively working with the material in real time, with others by their side.

Collaboration unlocks powerful learning benefits. It enhances understanding and retention. When learners must explain, troubleshoot, or build something with peers, their comprehension deepens. It sharpens critical thinking. Engaging with diverse perspectives stretches their worldview and challenges assumptions. And it builds essential social and professional skills – communication, feedback, problem-solving, and accountability – that stick long after your program ends.

There's also an emotional dimension. When learners see others grappling with similar challenges, it normalizes the process. They stop hiding. They start showing up. Group momentum is contagious: it fuels motivation and sustains engagement.

Your role is to create the container for that collaboration. When you do, your clients stop being passive *recipients* and become active *participants* in their own growth.

Pillar four: coaching – personalized support that moves the needle

Even with strong content, a thriving community, and collaborative momentum, there will always be moments when your clients need something more: a moment of clarity, a breakthrough conversation, or help with a challenge they're not ready to voice in public.

That's where coaching enters the equation – not as a scalable group tactic, but as *personalized, one-to-one support.*

This is where you shift from leader of the group to trusted guide for the individual. It's where your client feels truly seen. Where the invisible blocks surface. Where you help them translate ideas into action, tailored to their context, goals, and pace.

This isn't about spending endless hours in back-to-back sessions. With the Hybrid Authority Formula, coaching doesn't carry the full weight of transformation – it *complements* the rest of the experience. That's what makes it sustainable.

Even brief, focused touchpoints – like milestone reviews, voice notes, or laser strategy sessions – can unlock profound progress. When integrated into a broader hybrid structure, coaching becomes the accelerant, not the lifeline.

And for your clients? It's often the moment that makes everything else click. The reassurance that their experience matters.

The guidance that turns potential into performance. The nudge that moves them forward when they would've otherwise stalled.

It's not about *more* access. It's about the *right kind* of access. When done well, coaching becomes a surgical strike of value – and the final piece in a transformational learning journey.

The hybrid blend in action

When these four elements – content, community, collaboration, and coaching – come together, you don't just have a program. You have what we call a Hybrid Authority Experience.

It's a learning environment that is both structured and flexible. One that empowers learners to move at their own pace while staying deeply connected to others. It provides consistent access to your expertise yet gives clients agency in their own transformation. And perhaps most powerfully – it positions *you* not just as a coach or creator, but as the architect of an ecosystem. One that can scale, evolve, and grow without pulling you further into the grind.

This is more than a smart delivery method. It's a positioning strategy. A client experience strategy. A sustainability strategy. It elevates your brand while expanding your impact. And yes – it's your path to building a business that feels as good on the inside as it looks on the outside.

Because authority doesn't come from how much you teach or how many hours you coach. It comes from the results your clients achieve and the experience they have along the way. When transformation is baked into every layer of your offer, your reputation doesn't just grow – it compounds.

WHAT'S NEXT?

You now understand why traditional digital learning models fall short – and why transformation demands more than just curriculum, content, or clever branding.

In the next part, we'll explore the first of the four pillars of the Hybrid Authority Formula: **content**. Not as a library of lessons, but as a strategic, catalytic force that moves your learners forward.

Part II

CONTENT: BUILDING YOUR FOUNDATION

"

One of the greatest benefits of online learning is that it allows people to discover at their own pace, and in their own way.

Daphne Koller[3]

"

---

3   Daphne Koller has consistently advocated for the benefits of online education, particularly its capacity to offer personalized, self-paced learning experiences. See her TED Talk 'What We're Learning from Online Education.'

Your knowledge isn't the bottleneck.
Your delivery model is.

Before you can scale anything, you start here: designing your **digital twin** – a structured, scalable version of your brilliance. This isn't about dumping videos into a portal. It's about crafting content that drives clarity, sparks action, and becomes the foundation for the transformation ahead.

This part clarifies what content is needed in a hybrid experience, and why it's not just about what you teach, but how you build momentum.

4

Your digital twin: scale without sacrificing depth

Let's begin by rethinking one of the most important assets in your business: your time.

As an expert, your time is what you've always traded. One session at a time. One Zoom call at a time. One delivery cycle at a time. It's how you've built your reputation. It's how you've served clients, created impact, and made your income.

But here's the problem with that model: it doesn't scale. It can't. No matter how much demand you generate or how high your prices climb, eventually you reach the limit of what you can give. And if every result you create for a client depends on you being live, present, and involved, you've created a business that grows in direct proportion to your exhaustion.

That's the trap. And the way out of it is the 'digital twin.'

There comes a point in every expert's journey where being good at what you do is no longer enough. Your calendar's full, your clients are getting results, and from the outside, everything looks like it's working. But inside, you're stretched. And scaling feels impossible without sacrificing either the depth of your work or your sanity.

That's when you realize: the real limitation isn't your capacity. It's your delivery model.

You don't need to do more. You need to duplicate what already works – without having to show up live every time. That's where your digital twin comes in.

What a digital twin is – and isn't

Your digital twin isn't just a collection of content. It's not a video course. It's not your notes turned into slides. It's not a library of resources dumped into a portal. A digital twin is a strategic asset. It's a designed, structured, and scalable version of your expertise that can deliver clarity, direction, and momentum – without relying on your presence in the room.

This chapter is about the what and why of that shift. Not the tech. Not the formats. Not the production checklist. But the deeper strategic lens you need to step into if you want your knowledge to move beyond you, and still retain its power.

Because without a digital twin, you're not building leverage. You're just building dependence. And that dependence – on your energy, your time, your availability – will always cap your impact, your income, and your ability to grow.

Let's explore why that changes now.

So, what exactly *is* a digital twin?

It's the teachable expression of your expertise, packaged in a way that others can engage with independently. It's how your thinking, your methods, your unique lens on solving a problem are codified into something that clients can follow, implement, and benefit from, even when you're not involved in real time.

It's not a recording of you delivering a masterclass.

It's not a folder of PDFs.

It's not a 'just-in-case' content drop for people who missed the call.

A true digital twin is purposefully created to replicate the best of your teaching in a way that can stand on its own. It's your intellectual property, distilled. Your transformation method, clarified. It's a deliberate system that helps people get results, consistently and independently.

And that word – consistently – is the point.

When you deliver everything live, consistency is impossible. You might explain something better on Tuesday than you did on Monday. You might miss a nuance with one group that you nailed with another. Your energy fluctuates. Your availability shifts. Your delivery, no matter how experienced you are, is still subject to human variability.

Your digital twin doesn't have bad days. It doesn't forget a point. It doesn't rush because a session is running over time. It delivers the same clear message, the same structured insight, the same thought-out progression – every single time.

It's not about perfection. It's about precision.

That's what makes it a twin. Not a replica of your personality, but a refined, distilled expression of your process that works whether you're there or not.

A signal you can't ignore

If you've been delivering your expertise live – whether in workshops, coaching sessions, or consulting engagements – you've probably had the same thought more than once: 'I've explained this exact concept 20 times this week.'

That thought isn't just fatigue speaking. It's a signal.

It's telling you that your knowledge is ready to be documented. That your process is ready to be captured. That you've said something often enough, with consistent results, that it's time to turn that insight into an asset.

This is where most experts get stuck. They know they should 'create content,' but the idea feels overwhelming. What do I include? What format should I use? What if I say it wrong? What if it doesn't land?

But the real question to ask isn't, 'How do I record this?' The real question is, 'What would it take to make this repeatable?'

Because repeatability is the key to leverage. When your knowledge is repeatable, it becomes deployable. Reusable. Trainable. Valuable.

That's the shift. Not more content for the sake of content, but the kind of content that captures your process so clearly, it starts working for you – even when you're not working.

From bottleneck to backbone

If you're still operating in a delivery model where you are the asset – where the results depend on you being live, guiding the conversation, giving the feedback, holding the room – then you're stuck in what we call the 'exertion economy.'

The more you earn, the more you must do. The more clients you help, the more time you spend. Your business grows, but so does the demand on you. Eventually, the only way to keep going is to either raise your prices or stretch yourself thinner. Neither feels sustainable. Both feel like a trade-off.

A digital twin breaks that cycle, because when your expertise becomes an asset – a productized, structured, independent body of knowledge – you stop being the bottleneck in your own business. You gain something most experts never experience: separation between value and presence.

You're still the source of the value, yes. But the delivery of that value no longer depends on your availability. That single shift makes scale possible. It gives you breathing room. It creates the conditions for a business that doesn't stall every time you want to take a break, run a live event, or go on holiday.

This isn't about replacing yourself. It's about respecting yourself. It's about ensuring the depth and quality of your work isn't tied to how much stamina you have on any given day.

And that's how your digital twin becomes more than content. It becomes infrastructure.

Authority through systemisation

When your digital twin is in place, something else shifts – something subtle, but powerful.

You stop being seen as someone who just delivers sessions. You become someone who has built a system. That perception changes everything. It changes how clients see you. It changes how partners talk about you. It changes how buyers engage with you.

Experts who deliver sessions are respected. But experts who build systems are trusted to create consistent results. They're viewed not just as talented professionals, but as authorities. As the ones who have cracked a process, mapped a method, and designed a framework that others can follow.

This elevates you from consultant to creator. From knowledge-holder to knowledge-leader.

Authority sells. Authority creates demand, drives referrals, and opens doors to corporate contracts, licensing deals, and long-term partnerships.

You don't build authority by posting more on LinkedIn. You build it by showing that your work is codified. That your expertise has been shaped into something people can use, trust, and apply – without needing you to repeat yourself every time.

That's what a digital twin communicates. Not just that you know your stuff, but that you've built something others can rely on.

That's a whole new level of positioning.

Breathing room, at last

Beyond the strategy, beyond the authority, there's something more human underneath all of this: relief. Because the moment you create a digital twin is the moment you start to feel some breathing room again.

You no longer dread another round of onboarding, because you know your foundational thinking is already captured. You no longer feel pressure to 'perform' live for every new group, because you've built an experience that holds its own. You no longer feel like you must chase perfection in the moment, because the most important pieces of your work are already done, thought through, refined, recorded, and delivered with clarity.

There's a peace that comes with that. A confidence. A grounded sense of, 'Yes – I've built something real.'

It's not just freeing for you. It's reassuring for your clients.

They know they're not getting a version of your ideas that depends on your energy. They're getting the version you designed on purpose. The version that works. The version crafted for results.

That's when your business starts to feel like it has a backbone. That's when it stops being you, juggling and dancing to keep everything going – and starts being something solid. Structured. Strategic. Scalable.

That's the power of a digital twin.

Laying the groundwork for what comes next

So, no – it's not just content. It's not a passive info dump. It's not a placeholder for the 'real' experience. And it's not a downgrade from live interaction.

Your digital twin is the gateway to every other part of your offer. It makes your delivery scalable. It creates consistency across every client journey. It's the foundation that makes deeper engagement possible because it gives every learner a structured starting point.

But building a digital twin is only the first part of designing transformational content. Once your knowledge is captured and accessible, the next question is: how do your clients engage with it?

That's where we turn next – still within the **content** pillar – to explore the role of self-paced learning. Not just as a convenience, but as a powerful enabler of autonomy, access, and inclusivity.

Because the content you create can only work if it's delivered in a way that works for the learner.

5

The power of
self-paced learning

If your digital twin is the asset, self-paced learning is how that asset reaches your clients.

It's not just a convenient option or a way to 'catch up' between coaching calls. Self-paced learning is a deliberate and essential delivery mode that allows your content to do its job – on demand, on schedule, and at the pace that suits the learner.

In the Hybrid Authority Formula, self-paced learning isn't filler. It's foundational. It ensures your program works *beyond the calendar*, so that transformation is not limited by when someone can attend or how fast a group is moving.

It creates access. It provides structure. And when done right, it gives your learners the opportunity to build confidence before they step into coaching, collaboration, or community spaces.

The intentional creation of a flexible learning environment

Self-paced learning isn't about stepping back as the expert. It's about stepping forward in your design. It's the intentional creation of a learning environment that works because it's flexible.

One model; many learners

To understand the value of self-paced learning, you must start with one basic reality: your clients do not all learn the same way. Some will be driven, focused, and eager to move fast. Others will need space to reflect, revisit, and go slowly. Some will binge content in one weekend. Others will work through it in short bursts over several weeks. And nearly all of them are managing their learning around other priorities – businesses, jobs, kids, daily responsibilities.

A rigid, schedule-bound model excludes that diversity.

Self-paced learning, when integrated into the core of your program, says: 'you're welcome here – regardless of your pace, schedule, or starting point.'

That inclusiveness is not just a nice-to-have. It's essential for scale.

Laying the groundwork for real-time learning

But it's not just about pace. It's about preparedness. When self-paced content is used as the first step in a hybrid experience, it lays the groundwork for everything else that follows.

It introduces the key concepts, language, frameworks, and tools your clients need to participate in group sessions, collaborate with peers, or receive coaching. It gives them context. It creates a shared foundation. It ensures that when they show up in your live environments, they're not starting from zero.

They come equipped. Or at the very least, they come oriented.

And that changes the quality of everything else.

Self-paced learning doesn't replace the live experience. It prepares people to make the most of it.

Building ownership and momentum

It also shifts the relationship your clients have with your content.

In a live-first model, clients often rely on the coach to 'walk them through it.' That creates dependency. It limits ownership. It trains clients to wait for an explanation rather than develop confidence in exploring the material themselves.

However, when your program is designed to begin with self-paced content, it trains the learner in a different way. It invites them to take initiative. It builds trust in the material and in their own ability to engage with it. It signals that learning is not something done *to* them, but something they do *for* themselves.

That shift – from passive to active engagement – creates momentum. And in a hybrid experience, momentum is everything.

Flexibility as a signal of inclusivity

When you build in self-paced flexibility, you're making a statement: 'you belong here – even if your pace is different.'

That's how you build programs that include, rather than exclude. That's how you honor neurodiversity, energy variability, and the unpredictable rhythms of adult life. And that's how you reduce the dropout rate – not with better motivation, but with better design.

Because when learners feel respected, they stay.

A complement, not a complete solution

Of course, self-paced learning also comes with limitations.

On its own, it doesn't create accountability. It doesn't generate interaction. And it doesn't give you real-time insight into where people are getting stuck.

That's why it can't be the *only* component of your delivery.

But when it's integrated intentionally – as part of the Hybrid Authority Formula – it doesn't have to do everything. It just must do its part.

And that part is critical. It creates the structure. It sets the tone. It lets your digital twin function as intended. And it ensures your learners achieve the clarity they need before moving into more collaborative or supported spaces.

Free your time without losing impact

From a business perspective, self-paced learning does something else: it unlocks scalability without compromising quality. When your content can be delivered on demand – without needing to be taught live each time – you remove the single biggest bottleneck in most expert businesses: *your* calendar.

You're no longer repeating the same foundational content in every group. You're not burning hours on one-to-one explanations. You're not exhausting yourself trying to deliver consistent experiences manually.

Instead, your energy goes where it's needed most: into live support, deeper conversations, personalized coaching, and program improvement. And none of that comes at the expense of your clients' experience – because they're already engaging with a well-designed, self-paced foundation.

It all starts here

Self-paced learning is not about stepping back as the expert. It's about stepping forward as the designer of the experience. It's about recognizing that transformation doesn't begin on a live call. It begins the moment your client encounters your ideas, and feels like they can understand and apply them.

When that moment happens on their own time, without pressure or comparison, it creates emotional safety. And from that safety comes confidence. And from that confidence comes engagement.

That's the role of self-paced learning.

It doesn't replace support. It earns it. It doesn't remove interaction. It makes it more valuable. And it doesn't reduce your presence. It expands your reach – without compromising the quality of what you offer.

That's not just a design decision. It's a leadership decision.

And it's one of the most powerful choices you can make when building a transformational hybrid program.

6

Content as catalyst, not curriculum

There's a common misconception that content *is* the program. That if you build enough modules, cover enough topics, and pack in enough information, your learners will automatically get great results.

But information alone isn't transformation. More lessons won't fix a disengaged learner. More hours of content won't solve the problem of implementation. And a heavier curriculum does not equal a better experience.

This chapter will reframe that thinking.

Because in the Hybrid Authority Formula, content is not the curriculum. It's the **catalyst**.

It's the starting point, not the centerpiece. It's what sparks momentum – not what sustains it on its own. And until you understand the strategic role your content plays inside a hybrid experience, it's easy to overbuild, over teach, and overload the very people you're trying to serve.

So, let's draw a line between content that *informs* and content that *activates*.

The real purpose of your content

In a traditional course model, content is often treated like the product. The more there is, the more value it's seen to hold. Hours of video. Dozens of lessons. PDFs upon PDFs. A comprehensive knowledge vault.

But the goal of the Hybrid Authority Formula isn't to build a content library. It's to design a **learning journey**. And in that journey, content serves a specific purpose: to create *movement*.

Not movement through a checklist. Movement in mindset. Movement in clarity, capability, and direction.

Content is there to take the learner from confusion to confidence – from 'I don't know where to start' to 'I can see the path.'

That's the role it plays. And when you define your content this way, it changes what you create, how much you create, and how you position it inside the broader experience.

Your job isn't to cover everything. Your job is to clear the path. Content holds the torch.

Content should create energy, not exhaustion

One of the easiest ways to derail a hybrid program is to overload it with too much material. Not because the material isn't useful, but because the learner can't find the momentum to work through it all.

This happens when content is positioned as the *main event*. When the assumption is that results come from consuming everything in the portal before engaging anywhere else.

But people don't join your program because they want more information. They join because they want movement. Traction. Relief. Direction.

Content should support that desire, not stall it.

When your content is used as a catalyst, it creates a surge of energy. It simplifies complexity. It gives people a sense of progress, even if they're only partway through. It shows them that change is possible – not someday, but right now.

This is where confidence is built. Not at the end of the module series, but in the first few moments where something finally makes sense.

That kind of clarity makes people lean in. It makes them want to show up to the coaching call. It gives them something to share in the community. It anchors them in the experience.

That's not a lesson. That's a launch.

The shift from teaching to priming

In many programs, content is created with a teaching mindset:

- 'What do they need to learn?'
- 'How do I explain this in detail?'
- 'What examples do I include to be thorough?'

That's fine – if your only goal is to educate.

But if your goal is to activate, the better question is: *'What do they need to know to take action?'*

The purpose of content in a hybrid model isn't to teach everything. It's to get your learners ready for what comes next. Ready for the coaching conversation. Ready for the implementation session. Ready to test, to build, to share, to reflect.

This isn't about reducing depth. It's about being strategic in your sequence. It's about making sure your content doesn't become a bottleneck. That people aren't stuck in endless consumption when what they need is application.

Think of your content as the primer coat – not the final paint. It prepares the surface. It makes everything else land better. Without it, the rest of the experience doesn't stick.

What happens when your content does its job

When your content plays the right role in your hybrid experience, the impact is immediate and noticeable.

Clients arrive in coaching calls already thinking critically about their situation.

They enter the community with relevant, informed questions.

They show up to collaboration sessions with drafts, outlines, or half-built assets – ready for input, not instruction.

And perhaps most importantly, they don't treat you as the oracle. They treat you as the strategist. Because they've already interacted with your ideas, frameworks, and guidance on their own. They're not waiting for direction. They're building with it.

That changes the posture of your whole program. It turns your time from reactive to proactive. It elevates the level of conversation. It deepens the engagement. And it ensures your live delivery adds *value*, not just repetition.

When content does its job, everything else becomes easier.

Content that connects, not just informs

There's also a human layer here that often gets missed.

When someone works through content and feels seen by it – when it feels like it was designed for the problems they're facing – they become emotionally invested. They trust the process. They trust you. And they trust themselves more, because they're not just receiving information – they're connecting with it.

This is how you build momentum before anyone even joins a live session. Before they say a word in the community. Before they ask their first question in coaching.

They already feel like they're part of something that gets them. That's what keeps them in the experience. That's what turns a program from useful into transformational.

Why less content creates more value

It's worth saying clearly: volume does not equal value.

The goal of content in a hybrid program is not to say everything – it's to say the *right* things, in the right order, to create the right shift.

When you try to teach everything inside your modules, you rob your live environments of oxygen. You overload your learners. You bury the most important insights under a mountain of material.

But when you create content that acts as a catalyst – short, sharp, clear, and sequenced with intention – you give the rest of your experience room to breathe. You create space for reflection. Space for conversation. Space for coaching to be responsive instead of repetitive.

And your learners feel the difference. They don't feel like they're trying to survive your program. They feel like they're moving through it with clarity, ownership, and confidence.

Content is the starting line, not the destination

It's easy to fall into the trap of thinking your content is the hero of your program. That if you just make it good enough, thorough enough, beautiful enough, the results will follow.

But in a hybrid model, your content isn't the destination. It's the starting line.

It's what brings people into motion. It's what prepares them to show up in your community. To collaborate. To be coached. To do the work that truly drives change.

That's what content is for. That's the role it plays. Not to complete the journey, but to begin it well.

And when you approach your content with that mindset, everything else you build becomes more powerful.

Your community becomes more engaged.

Your coaching becomes more effective.

Your learners become more empowered.

Because the content didn't try to do everything. It did what it was meant to do: create clarity, spark momentum, and prime the experience.

That's what makes it a catalyst.

WHAT'S NEXT?

Powerful content can activate momentum.
But information alone doesn't create
lasting change.

In the next part, we explore the second pillar
of hybrid learning: **community** – the invisible
engine that supports identity, motivation,
and belonging.

Because people don't just learn content.
They learn *together*.

Part III

COMMUNITY: LEARNING TOGETHER, NOT ALONE

"

We are social beings, and our brains grow in a social environment.

Eric Jensen[4]

"

---

4   Eric Jensen is a former teacher and leading expert in brain-based learning, known for his work on how neuroscience informs education and engagement. He frequently highlights the social nature of learning and the role of environment in brain development.

No one learns in a vacuum. When your learners feel connected, supported, and seen, they engage more deeply and stay longer.

In this part, we unpack how to design an intentional community that fosters belonging, resilience, and insight.

You'll learn how to create the kind of shared space that turns passive learners into active participants – and content into lived experience.

7

Content informs, community transforms

Let's start with a truth that every expert feels but few admit: creating great content is no longer enough.

You've built something rich with insights. Maybe you've spent hours scripting videos, writing resources, designing inter-active quizzes, even building a beautiful platform. You've taken everything you know and packaged it into something scalable, something that delivers your genius without you having to show up live every time.

And yet – something's missing.

Your learners might start strong, but their motivation fades. Completion rates stall. The energy you normally feel when you teach live is absent. You keep wondering, 'How can I get people to actually use what I'm giving them?'

Here's the shift to make: if content informs, it's community that transforms.

Why information isn't enough

Content delivers information. It introduces ideas. It builds awareness. But information alone rarely leads to meaningful, lasting transformation. Especially when that information is delivered in isolation.

Without a community context, content often becomes passive. Learners consume, but they don't engage. They understand, but they don't implement. They value your method, but they struggle to apply it in their world.

In fact, one of the most common mistakes in the online education space is overestimating what content can do on its own. Just because someone has access to the knowledge doesn't mean they'll integrate it. Just because they've completed a module doesn't mean it changed them.

Real learning happens when people are invited to wrestle with ideas. When they see how others interpret the same message. When they test it in action, compare notes, get feedback, and reflect aloud. And none of that happens inside a static video player.

Content lays the foundation. But the house is built in community.

Why we learn better together

As human beings, we're wired to learn in relationship with others. Learning has always been social – long before we had platforms or frameworks or course portals.

Think back to how humans have passed down knowledge across generations. Not through PDFs or PowerPoint decks, but through stories, rituals, apprenticeships, shared work.

We've always learned best in environments where we're seen, heard, and supported. Where we belong.

That hasn't changed. What's changed is the medium.

Digital learning often separates us from that social context. And while the flexibility of online delivery is a gift, it also creates distance between learners, between the learner and the expert, and between the content and the real-world conversations it's meant to spark.

It's in community that learners find validation, discover nuance, and stay accountable. It's where they get stuck, get challenged, and get unstuck – together. It's where ideas are clarified, and learning becomes more than intellectual; it becomes personal.

This isn't just theory – it's backed by decades of learning science.

Albert Bandura's social learning theory revealed that people learn by watching others, modeling behaviors, and receiving reinforcement. Vygotsky introduced the Zone of Proximal Development, showing that learners can achieve far more when they're supported by peers and guides than they can alone.[5] We learn better in community.

But you don't need to dive into educational theory to see this in action. Just think about your own learning. When have you truly shifted your thinking or behavior? Was it after watching a module, or in the conversations that followed?

---

5   Lev Vygotsky was a Soviet psychologist best known for his theory of social development and the concept of the Zone of Proximal Development, which illustrates how learners progress more effectively with the support of more knowledgeable others, such as peers, teachers, or mentors.

The impact of isolation on learners

If we ignore community, we leave transformation up to chance.

The learner who feels isolated is more likely to fall behind. Not because they're lazy or unmotivated, but because they're human. Without touchpoints, without a sense of shared momentum, the noise of life takes over. Work deadlines. Family obligations. Decision fatigue. Distractions.

When there's no social container, there's no urgency. When there's no sense of shared movement, there's no pressure to follow through. And when there's no space to process aloud, reflect with others, or hear different perspectives, even the best ideas can stagnate.

This is why completion rates in online courses hover at depressingly low levels. The content isn't the problem. The delivery model is. It's designed for isolation, and isolation doesn't sustain transformation.

The solution? Don't bolt on community. Build it in.

Designing community as part of the experience

In the Hybrid Authority Formula, community isn't an add-on. It's a core pillar. Just like content, collaboration, and coaching, it plays a distinct role in the learning journey.

Where content delivers the 'what,' community supports the 'why now,' 'why this matters,' and 'what does this look like in my world?'

You're not just delivering information. You're designing an environment. A container. A culture. And that culture is where learning sticks.

Community provides emotional safety. It builds shared momentum. It transforms your program from a transactional product into a living, breathing experience.

It's not about the size of the community or the tech behind it. It's about the intention with which it's designed.

Even a small cohort of learners – if given the right prompts, rhythms, and permissions – can create a profound learning culture.

Community creates accountability. Not through deadlines or fear, but through connection. It's one thing to skip a module. It's another to skip a call knowing others are waiting to hear your insights, your questions, your breakthroughs. Community invites responsibility – not just to the content, but to each other.

Your role isn't just to teach – it's to host

When you build a hybrid program, your role shifts. You're not just an instructor delivering content. You're a host creating space. You're the architect of a shared learning experience.

And like any good host, your job is to curate the guest list, set the tone, and guide the flow. You don't need to be the center of attention, but you do need to hold the container.

This might feel unfamiliar if you're usually the expert in the spotlight. But when you start designing for community, your authority isn't diminished. It's amplified. You become the trusted guide who not only knows the map but creates the environment in which others can meaningfully explore it.

You become the reason your learners stay – not because you have all the answers, but because you've built a space where it's safe to ask the right questions.

That's what sets hybrid learning apart from traditional online courses. It's not just about delivering content – it's about designing for change. And change doesn't happen in isolation. It happens in community.

This isn't optional

You might be thinking, 'This sounds great in theory, but does it really make a difference?'

It does. And not just for your learners – but for you.

Programs with active communities retain learners longer. They produce more success stories. They generate more referrals. They create more brand equity. Why? Because they don't just deliver a product – they deliver an experience. An experience that's shared. An experience that matters.

When learners connect, they don't just learn more – they care more. And when they care more, they finish more, achieve more, and talk about it more.

But here's the bonus most experts don't expect: community also makes *your* job easier.

When it's designed well, your community becomes self-sustaining. You don't have to respond to every comment or provide every insight. The group starts to answer its own questions, spark its own momentum, and reinforce your teachings without you having to hover. You become what we call a 'lazy facilitator' – not absent, but intentional. You create the conditions, then let the culture take over.

It's the difference between carrying every learner on your shoulders and creating a circle where they lift each other.

If you're aiming to scale transformation – not just access – community isn't optional.

So, if you've been pouring your energy into your content and wondering why it's not landing the way you hoped, this is your invitation to shift.

Stop thinking of community as the wrapper. Start designing it as a foundational pillar.

Because in this new era of expert-led education, the programs that succeed aren't the ones with the fanciest production or the most modules. They're the ones that create a place to belong. A space to grow. A community to learn *with*, not just *from*.

And that's what turns information into transformation.

8

The psychology of engagement

There's a reason your learners perk up the moment they're in a room – or even a breakout Zoom – with others. It's not just about interaction. It's about how we're wired. Human brains are social brains. And if you want your learning experiences to create real, lasting transformation, you need to understand this truth at a deeper level: we don't learn alone.

In the previous chapter, we explored the powerful difference community makes. But let's now go beneath the surface and look at why that's the case. Why does learning with others accelerate growth? Why do conversations cement understanding? Why do peer environments drive momentum better than any fancy course dashboard ever could?

To answer that, we need to look at the science.

And not the cold, clinical kind. We're talking about the psychology of motivation. The neuroscience of connection. The social scaffolding that makes learning not only effective, but inevitable.

We learn by watching others

Let's start with the work of psychologist Albert Bandura.

In the 1960s, Bandura introduced the concept of social learning theory. The idea was groundbreaking for its time – and is still underappreciated today in the design of many digital programs.

Bandura's core insight? People learn by observing others. Not just by hearing about a concept or reading an explanation. But by seeing it in action. Watching someone else model the behavior, walk through the process, or wrestle with the idea. And then mimicking, adapting, and personalizing it.

This happens in classrooms. It happens in workplaces. And it happens – when designed well – in your hybrid programs.

Bandura called this 'observational learning,' and it's incredibly powerful. Not just because it transfers knowledge, but because it bypasses cognitive overload. When we watch someone else apply a concept, it becomes real. We see nuance. We anticipate challenges. We feel capable, because we're not starting from scratch – we're starting from a reference point.

You might already do this instinctively when you record a demo video or walk through a case study. But the opportunity becomes tenfold when you build a space where learners can see each other do it too. Where they're not just learning from you but learning from each other.

This is where social learning stops being a theory and starts being an organic driver of growth and connection in your program.

Where learning comes alive

Russian psychologist Lev Vygotsky added another dimension to this conversation with his idea of the 'Zone of Proximal

Development.' Don't let the term scare you off – it's a simple but profound idea.

Vygotsky argued we all have two learning zones:

- The first is what we can do on our own – our current level of mastery.
- The second is what we can't yet do, even with help.

But between those two is a sweet spot: what we 'can' do with the support of someone more experienced. That might be a coach, a peer, a mentor, or a group. This is the Zone of Proximal Development.

ZONE OF PROXIMAL DEVELOPMENT

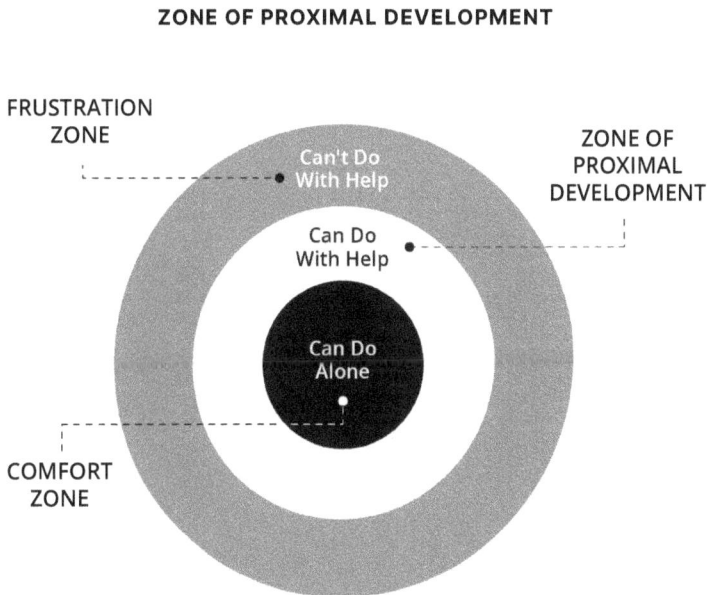

And this is exactly where your learners are when they enter your program.

They've signed up because they want to grow, but they're not there yet. If they could do it on their own, they wouldn't have signed up. But if it felt entirely impossible, they wouldn't have joined either.

They're right on the edge. Ready to move. Needing support.

And that support doesn't have to come solely from you. Some of the most potent movement happens when learners help each other. When someone says, 'I struggled with that too – here's what worked for me.' Or, 'I applied that framework like this – would that approach fit your context?'

That's not just encouraging – it's developmental. It pushes them through the zone. It builds confidence, not just knowledge. And it creates something no video or worksheet can: movement.

Motivation is also social

Here's another myth that needs busting: that motivation is purely individual.

It's not.

Motivation is contagious. It echoes. It spreads around a group.

Think about it. Have you ever walked into a quiet room and felt yourself shrinking to match the energy? Or entered a buzzing group and suddenly felt more alert, more engaged, more alive?

That's social motivation.

When learners see others engaging, they're more likely to engage. When they hear someone else commit to a goal, they're more likely to articulate their own goals. When they watch someone take imperfect action, they're more likely to try too.

This isn't accidental. It's psychological.

Daniel Pink, in his research on motivation, breaks it down into three components: autonomy, mastery, and purpose.[6]

But what's often overlooked is how all three are fuelled by social interaction.

Autonomy flourishes when learners feel safe to choose their path – and that safety often comes from being part of a group that respects different approaches.

Mastery deepens when learners can benchmark against others – not competitively, but collaboratively. Seeing progress in others helps us believe in our own.

Purpose is amplified when you're not just growing for yourself, but contributing to a community. When you know your insight could help someone else. When you feel responsible for contributing to the group's energy.

This is why a hybrid learning experience without community doesn't just miss an element – it misses the motivational engine entirely.

Meaning-making is a group activity

One of the most underestimated parts of learning is meaning-making.

It's the process of taking content and turning it into something personal. Something relevant. Something that sticks.

And meaning is not made in isolation.

It's made in conversation.

---

6   Daniel Pink is an American author and speaker known for his research on motivation and behavior.

When learners are given the space to reflect aloud, to hear how others interpreted the same idea, to debate the value of an approach, they move from understanding to ownership. The content becomes theirs. It fits their world, not just yours.

This is why reflection prompts matter. Why dialogue beats monologue. Why your job as the expert isn't just to 'tell' but to create space for 'sense-making.'

Think of your program not as a conveyor belt of information, but as a campfire. You spark the fire. You bring the first stories. But it's in the shared warmth, the echoed insights, the back-and-forth, that the real power emerges.

You're not just delivering – you're designing

All of this leads to a critical reframe as a coach, consultant, or educator using the Hybrid Authority Formula. Your job is not just to deliver learning. Your job is to design conditions where learning becomes inevitable.

And social learning is one of those conditions.

This doesn't mean you need to run group calls every day or build a 24/7 community space. It means being intentional about interaction. It means recognizing that transformation isn't just about content quality – it's about context. Who is in the room. How they're invited to contribute. What norms you establish. What culture you cultivate.

When you design a program culture where social learning is normal, expected, and celebrated, everything changes. Participation goes up. Implementation goes deeper. And your learners don't just complete the program – they grow through it.

Building a bridge back to real life

Learning doesn't matter if it stays locked in the program. Your goal isn't just to teach – it's to create transformation that travels beyond the course.

And one of the best predictors of whether that happens is whether your learners had to explain it, explore it, and use it socially 'inside' your program.

When people are asked to articulate what they've learned to others, they retain more. When they see how others are applying it, they're more likely to apply it themselves. When they get used to having real conversations about the work, they're far more likely to keep those conversations outside your program.

That's how you create ripple effects. Not by overloading content, but by designing for interaction.

Social learning isn't a theory from a dusty textbook. It's a design principle. A commitment. Learners don't just need information. They need each other.

When you embrace that, your programs stop being content libraries and start becoming ecosystems.

Places where knowledge grows, spreads, evolves.

Places where learning doesn't just happen – it multiplies.

9

The power of belonging

Let's talk about something that rarely shows up in course outlines, but quietly determines whether your learners engage,
participate, and ultimately transform: *belonging.*

It's the bridge between information and identity. It's the invisible thread that makes a learning space feel safe, relevant, and
resonant. And when you build your programs using the Hybrid
Authority Formula, it's one of the most potent – and often
overlooked – forces in your design toolkit.

You've probably felt it yourself. The moment you join a room
virtual or otherwise – and instantly sense you're welcome there.
When people talk like you, think like you, or at the very least
'see' you. Not as a username or a client or another enrolment,
but as a human being with a story and a voice.

That's belonging. And without it, even the best content can
fall flat.

'Do I fit here?'

Here's something most learners will never say out loud, but they're feeling it the moment they enter your program:

'Do I fit here?'

Not in terms of the technical level or curriculum relevance. That's the surface layer.

They're wondering if they'll be understood. If they'll be judged. If they'll have to prove their worth. If they'll be allowed to speak, to be honest, to stumble, to ask questions without shame.

If they'll matter.

And if the answer is *no* – if they don't feel seen or safe or included – they will quietly withdraw. Not dramatically. They'll just stop logging in. Stop engaging. Stop showing up with their full energy. Not because your content isn't valuable. But because the space doesn't feel like theirs.

That's the silent churn most programs never trace back to its root. It's not the modules. It's the missing emotional container. It's the absence of belonging.

Whether you've consciously designed it or not, your program has a culture. Every learning environment sends signals – about who belongs, how to behave, what's celebrated, what's tolerated, and what's ignored.

Is that culture inclusive, empowering, and participatory? Or is it silent, passive, and performative?

As the creator of a hybrid learning experience, you're not just building curriculum. You're building culture. From the first welcome message to the language in your calls to the way you respond to a vulnerable share, you're modeling what matters.

When learners see that their identity is not just accepted but valued, when they hear others speak their language or name their unspoken struggles, something clicks.

They don't just consume your content. They connect to it. They claim it. And they begin to reshape who they are through it. That's the power of belonging.

Where the transformation deepens

We often think of learning as cognitive. Something that happens in the mind.

But transformation doesn't come from information. It comes from an identity shift.

And identity is shaped in relation to others.

When learners see people like them succeeding, contributing, and experimenting, they start to expand what's possible for themselves. Not theoretically. Viscerally. The subconscious message becomes: 'People like me do things like this.'

That's identity integration. And it's the cornerstone of sustained behavioral change.

Belonging creates the conditions for that shift.

When you design a space where learners see their values reflected, their backgrounds respected, their voices invited, they begin to let go of the guardedness that keeps them in performance mode. They stop asking, 'What do I need to do to fit in?' and start asking, 'What do I want to do next?'

One of the markers of a strong learning community is that people stop trying to impress and start trying to connect. They don't need to show up with the *right* answer. They show up with *their* answer. Their reflection. Their messy thinking.

They're fully present.

That presence is only possible when the emotional cost of participation is low. When learners trust that they'll be met with curiosity, not critique. When sharing is encouraged, not just tolerated.

You can't force this. But you can foster it.

It starts by being human yourself. Sharing your story. Naming your missteps. Using language that signals care, not correction. Inviting stories, not just responses.

The more psychologically present you are, the more your learners feel they can be too.

This is where the transformation deepens. Not because you delivered more content, but because you delivered a different context where their evolving identity can take root.

Not all engagement looks the same

One of the most common misconceptions in online learning communities is that the loudest learners are the most engaged. But in every cohort, there are participants who will engage quietly. They may never comment. They may not join live calls. But they're there. Listening. Absorbing. Reflecting. Applying.

These learners are sometimes dismissed as 'lurkers' – but in educational theory, there's a more generous and accurate term: **legitimate peripheral participants**.

Coined by Jean Lave and Etienne Wenger, this idea recognizes that newcomers to any community often learn by observing first. They take in the norms, the language, the dynamics. They learn 'through the edges,' not the center. That participation is still meaningful.

Many of these quiet learners end up making significant progress behind the scenes. They're tuning into the collective energy. They're internalizing insights. They're shaping their identity in ways that aren't immediately visible.

And then, sometimes months later, they resurface with a story that reminds you: presence isn't always loud.

This is why your job as a program leader isn't to force everyone into the same engagement pattern – it's to signal belonging in all directions. To honor the talkers, the thinkers, the questioners, the notetakers. All of them are here. All of them are learning.

Tools don't create belonging

A lot of course creators make the mistake of thinking that adding a community platform – like a Facebook group or a Circle space – 'is' the community.

But tools don't create belonging. Culture does.

Belonging is felt, not announced. It's the energy in a group thread. The tone of feedback. The way learners respond when someone shares a win or a wobble. The way people show up for each other.

These aren't accidental moments. They're the result of intention.

Of inviting people to share their stories early, not just their goals.

Of spotlighting different voices, not just the loudest ones.

Of reinforcing that this is a space for growth, not for comparison.

Belonging is built through repetition, trust, and the small interactions that turn a group of strangers into a community.

You don't need a thousand people for this. You just need the right cues, the right rhythms, and the right leadership.

The bridge to what comes next

When learners feel like they belong, they don't just learn more. They take more risks. They speak more freely. They make bolder decisions. They act – not because they're being pushed, but because they're being held.

Belonging is what allows learners to cross the bridge from who they were to who they're becoming. It's what transforms your program from a place they visit to a place they make their own.

And that emotional resonance doesn't disappear when the program ends. It travels with them.

So, if you're wondering why one program creates superfans while another fades into the background – even with the same level of content – it's often this:

One built a culture. The other just delivered a course.

WHAT'S NEXT?

Community gives learners connection –
but connection alone doesn't guarantee
progress.

In the next part, we shift our focus to
collaboration: how shared implementation
environments create accountability, deepen
understanding, and move learners from
ideas to action.

Part IV

COLLABORATION: FROM KNOWING TO DOING

"

None of us is as smart as all of us.

Ken Blanchard[7]

"

---

7   Ken Blanchard is an American author, leadership expert, and co-author of *The One Minute Manager*. He is widely recognized for his work on team performance and servant leadership, and is known for emphasizing the power of collaboration.

Knowledge isn't power – *applied* knowledge is.

Content gives clarity. But collaboration builds capability.

This section explores how to create structured opportunities for learners to implement what they're learning **with others**. Whether it's group sprints, peer feedback, or co-working formats – collaboration turns ideas into output.

You'll learn how to design collaborative formats that create accountability, shared momentum, and deeper results.

10

The collective advantage: why momentum multiplies

If the community pillar is about 'learning together, not alone,' the collaboration pillar is about 'doing together, not alone.'

You've seen this in action: learners who are excited in theory but stuck in practice. They've consumed the content. They've nodded through the frameworks. They've bookmarked all the best insights. But when it comes to implementation, they hesitate.

They open the workbook. Stare at the prompt. Overthink the next step. Put it off.

It's not that they don't want results – they do. But like most humans, they struggle to act in isolation.

What changes the game is the presence of others.

Collaboration doesn't just add social texture to your program. It adds kinetic energy. It creates a rhythm of movement, a current that pulls learners forward – faster, deeper, and with far more staying power than they'd manage on their own.

This is the collective advantage.

It's not about groupthink. It's not about forcing people to do everything together.

It's about deliberately designing opportunities for learners to act in the presence of others, so that action becomes inevitable.

Action is contagious

When someone shares a plan in a group session, the person next to them starts drafting their own. When one learner posts a messy-but-done worksheet in the forum, others follow. When someone says, 'I'm testing this tomorrow,' it nudges others to get out of theory and into motion.

That's the social momentum effect.

We move faster when others are moving too. Not because we're trying to compete, but because the inertia of isolation has been replaced by the current of collaboration.

Think about the difference between reading a book on running and joining a running club. The book is helpful, but the club gets you moving. You don't need to lead the pack. You just need to lace up and show up.

The same is true for your learners.

When they work alone, every step requires willpower. When they work together, progress becomes normalized.

That's the multiplier effect of collaboration. It doesn't just support action. It normalizes it.

From passive knowing to active doing

One of the biggest threats to impact in a digital program is passive comprehension.

Your learners understand the material. They agree with the logic. They love the model. But they haven't applied it. The download hasn't become output. Insight hasn't become execution.

And it's not for lack of intelligence. It's for lack of integration.

Collaboration breaks that pattern.

When learners are asked to 'do' together – to problem-solve, to test, to build, to reflect in real time – they're forced to externalize their thinking. They must articulate decisions. Justify approaches. Iterate out loud.

And in doing so, they move from understanding to ownership.

It's one thing to understand a principle. It's another to work it through alongside peers. Hear their take. Compare interpretations. Watch it applied in real-world contexts you hadn't considered.

Collaboration exposes blind spots. It reinforces learning. And perhaps most importantly, it accelerates application. Because nothing speeds up implementation like knowing someone else is counting on you to show up with a draft, a reflection, or a deliverable.

The safety of shared struggle

There's a quiet relief in knowing you're not the only one still figuring it out.

Collaboration creates that kind of safety. The kind where people can show up mid-process, not just post-polish. Where it's okay to not have it all together. Where progress is celebrated over perfection.

This kind of environment makes it safer to try. Safer to ship. Safer to ask questions you might have hidden in a solo space.

Collaboration doesn't just move people forward. It gives them permission to 'move forward messily.' And in doing so, it gets them out of the paralysis of overthinking and into action.

Because when learners feel safe to take imperfect action, they take more action. And the more they act, the faster the transformation compounds.

Momentum becomes shared infrastructure

In a well-designed collaborative environment, the learners aren't just learning from you – they're also scaffolding the experience for each other.

One person's breakthrough becomes another person's shortcut.

One team's implementation creates a template others can adapt.

Collaboration builds collective assets. Shared language. Embedded norms. A rhythm of execution that becomes part of the program culture.

Soon, your learners are not just consuming from you – they're contributing to the learning ecosystem. They're not just recipients of value – they're part of the value engine itself.

This is where hybrid programs transcend a simple curriculum. They become movements.

And it doesn't require scale. A small, committed group with the right structure and purpose can generate more meaningful momentum than a hundred silent students behind login screens.

You become the conductor, not the workhorse

Here's the part that matters for you: when collaboration becomes a core pillar, not an afterthought, you're no longer carrying the full weight of every learner's progress.

You're designing the tempo. You're setting the cues. You're shaping the energy.

But the momentum? That's distributed.

You're not stuck trying to motivate one learner at a time. You're not constantly re-engaging or dragging people to the finish line.

The group helps itself move. And as the program leader, you get to shift into a new kind of authority – not the person who knows it all, but the person who's created the system that allows others to act powerfully.

That's what sustainable, scalable transformation looks like. Not you doing more, but the system you've designed doing the heavy lifting – because learners are now learning through each other, not just from you.

Why this isn't just a learning tactic

You might be tempted to think of collaboration as a tool. A learning strategy. A cool format to mix things up.

But it's more than that.

Collaboration is a principle. A commitment. A way of honoring the fact that learning isn't just about insight – it's about implementation. And implementation happens better, faster, and more consistently when it's done together.

In the Hybrid Authority Formula, collaboration isn't a feature. It's a foundational lever of transformation.

It's how your learners move from ideas to outcomes.

It's how your program becomes an accelerator, not a content library.

It's how you scale results – not by doing more yourself, but by designing for the collective advantage.

11

How to spark shared action

Collaboration doesn't happen by accident.

It's not enough to say, 'Work together' or 'Join the call' or 'Engage with your peers.' If there's no structure, no container, and no intention behind it, what you get is either surface-level interaction or nothing at all.

This is why formats matter.

The right format creates flow. It gives learners a reason to show up, a purpose for being there, and a rhythm that makes action feel inevitable. It transforms vague ideas into visible progress. It makes the experience feel alive.

But here's the thing: formats aren't about bells and whistles. They're not a way to make your program more entertaining. They're a tool to move people into motion.

Because in the Hybrid Authority Formula, content introduces, but collaboration integrates. And to drive integration at scale, you need the right containers for collective doing.

Formats that move

Let's look at the formats that do this best – not from a 'how to run them' perspective, but from a 'why they work' angle. What do these containers offer your learners that traditional consumption-based delivery can't?

Co-working sessions: the antidote to procrastination

Let's start with one of the simplest, yet most powerful formats: the live co-working session.

At first glance, it looks too basic to matter. No teaching. No slides. Just a group of learners on Zoom, muted, doing their own work – with check-ins at the start and end.

But here's what's really happening under the surface.

The learner who's been stuck in inertia suddenly has a reason to open the tab. The task they've been overthinking is actioned in a 60-minute window. The presence of others replaces the need for internal motivation.

This isn't about shared instruction – it's about shared discipline.

Co-working sessions work because they turn solo effort into shared momentum. They transform a task from 'I'll get to it' into 'I'm doing it right now.'

For programs built around implementation, co-working isn't filler. It's fuel.

It helps people cross the line between intention and execution. And it reinforces that progress doesn't always look like breakthroughs – it often looks like focused time, quietly spent, in good company.

Implementation weeks: turning insight into output

Another format that drives serious forward motion is the dedicated implementation sprint, often run as a themed 'week' or 'block' inside a program.

During this window, learning pauses. No new content. No new frameworks. Just space to apply what's already been taught – with live touchpoints, accountability, and peer visibility baked in.

Why does this work? Because one of the most common reasons learners fall behind isn't confusion – it's overwhelm. They're not stuck because the material is unclear. They're stuck because they haven't had the *space* to do the work.

Implementation weeks give them that space, without letting momentum go cold.

They send a powerful message: 'You're not here to just learn – you're here to build, apply, create, test, implement.' That message creates an internal shift. Learners stop being passive students and start acting like practitioners.

They roll up their sleeves. They make real progress. And they do it with the support and accountability of the group beside them.

Workshops: action-oriented, not just idea-driven

Live workshops are a staple in many programs, but not all workshops are created equal.

The workshops that move people forward are the ones that move the learner. Not just intellectually, but practically. These sessions aren't about transferring more information. They're about working through something together.

A live teardown. A group brainstorm. A real-time mapping session. A coaching room where ideas are stress-tested on the spot.

The magic of a good workshop isn't in the teaching – it's in the *doing inside the session.*

When you create space for learners to make real progress in the room (instead of walking away with another list of things to think about), you collapse the learning–action gap.

The ripple effect is huge.

Learners walk out of those sessions not just with insight, but with assets. Decisions made. Strategies clarified. Messaging drafted. Actions committed to.

It's no longer a *learning about.* It's a *learning through.*

That's what drives momentum.

Peer feedback rounds: making reflection relational

One of the most underestimated formats in hybrid delivery is peer review.

Most program creators are afraid to use it, worried that feedback will be unhelpful, off-track, or even demotivating. And yes, poor peer feedback can be counterproductive.

But well-structured peer feedback rounds are gold. They make learning visible.

When a learner must articulate what they see in someone else's work, they start to refine their own lens. When they provide thoughtful feedback on the work of others, they deepen their own understanding of the material. When they hear diverse perspectives, they see their blind spots – and their strengths – with new clarity.

Peer feedback rounds also normalize imperfection. They reinforce that the learning process is messy, iterative, and shared. They break the illusion that everyone else has it all figured out. And that psychological leveling effect makes progress feel possible.

Learners become less precious about their work. Less anxious about judgment. And more open to movement.

Because the goal isn't to be perfect – it's to be in motion, together.

Group sprints and challenges: collective energy, individual wins

When you want to inject momentum into your program, few things are more powerful than a shared challenge. A week to build something. A sprint to launch. A milestone to hit. A framework to apply, in full, in real life.

Challenges work because they create urgency *and* community. They give your learners a reason to act now and a tribe to act alongside.

The format matters less than the feeling: 'We're all doing this. Together. Right now.'

That's the shift that creates a wave of action. When learners know others are moving too, they stop waiting for perfect timing. They stop hiding behind one more video. They jump in. Test. Ship. Iterate. Win.

And when that wave hits, you get stories. Proof. Belief.

Why collaborative formats aren't optional

These formats aren't just delivery options. They're strategic containers. They take your curriculum out of the theoretical and into the transformational.

Collaboration, in practice, isn't just about interaction – it's about *doing with* structure. *Progress with* support. *Application with* company.

And without formats like these, learners are left to bridge that gap alone.

They might get there. But it will take longer. It will feel harder. And it will be lonelier.

When you design your program with collaborative formats baked in, you don't just help people learn. You help them move.

You don't just deliver information. You deliver acceleration.

And that's what positions your program as more than educational.

It becomes catalytic.

12

Designing a structure that scales

Collaboration sounds good in theory.

Shared learning. Real-time interaction. Peer accountability. Group momentum.

But if you've ever seen a group session descend into silence, confusion, or awkward small talk ... you know something else is also true: collaboration without structure doesn't create momentum. It creates mess.

It's a romantic idea, that people will naturally come together, share insights, support each other, and build beautiful things. But left to its own devices, collaboration isn't always functional. Without intentional design, it becomes an obstacle.

So, if you want your program to harness the power of collaborative learning – not just talk about it – you need more than enthusiasm. You need infrastructure.

Collaboration without chaos

The most powerful group experiences aren't spontaneous. They're planned and supported.

They have invisible rails that keep things moving. And when you get those rails in place, learners feel the freedom to engage fully, without the burden of figuring out how to do it.

Let's unpack what makes collaboration effective – and what causes it to fall apart.

Unclear roles create uneven contribution

One of the fastest ways to derail group learning is to leave responsibilities undefined. If learners don't know what they're expected to contribute, who's meant to lead, or what success looks like, they'll default to silence – or worse, domination by the most confident voice.

This isn't about creating hierarchy – it's about creating clarity. People thrive when they understand the boundaries of their participation. They show up more confidently when they know their role. They contribute more fully when expectations are clear.

Without that clarity, some learners hold back, unsure if they're stepping on toes. Others overstep, unintentionally silencing the group. The result? Resentment, hesitation, disengagement.

Effective collaboration isn't a free-for-all. It's a guided exchange.

And that guidance doesn't restrict contribution – it unlocks it.

The myth of organic participation

There's a belief that great conversations 'just happen' in communities and group sessions. But most of the time, they don't. Not without cues.

We forget that learners are arriving from different contexts, with different confidence levels, different communication styles, and different ideas of what's appropriate.

If you leave them to 'just engage,' what you usually get is hesitation. Or a few voices doing all the heavy lifting while the rest watch silently.

What changes that?

Structure.

Prompts. Time frames. Turn-taking. Visual anchors. Shared goals. Small groups instead of large ones. Asynchronous prep before live sessions. Opt-in formats for activities that could make learners vulnerable.

These are trust-builders. They tell your learners, 'You're safe here. You're supported here. You're not being dropped into the deep end – you're being guided through.'

And when people feel that? They show up.

Psychological safety is essential for group learning

We've talked about belonging in the context of community, but collaboration is where that belonging gets tested.

Working together involves exposure. You must share your thinking before it's perfect. Ask questions before you're sure. Offer ideas that might not land. Give feedback that might not be well received. Let others into your process before you've figured it all out.

That kind of openness is powerful – but it can also make learners vulnerable.

So if the environment doesn't feel safe, learners will play it small. They'll nod along. They'll coast. They'll pretend. And collaboration will fail.

Psychological safety isn't a fluffy concept. It's a foundation of performance in group learning.

It's what allows people to take risks. It's what gives them permission to be messy in public. And it's what keeps them in the program when the work gets uncomfortable – because they trust the space is strong enough to hold them.

As the program leader, you're the steward of that safety, not just through your facilitation but through the program design.

What are the norms? The rules of engagement? The social contracts in place?

Do people know how to ask for support? Are there clear mechanisms for feedback? Are difficult conversations modeled, so learners don't avoid them?

Psychological safety doesn't happen by announcement. It happens by design.

And without it, collaborative formats collapse under the weight of unspoken fear.

Boundaries create freedom

This is one of the great paradoxes of learning design: the more freedom you want your learners to feel, the more structure you need to create.

It sounds counterintuitive. Shouldn't freedom come from open space?

Not in the learning context. Open space without guidance feels like abandonment. It invites uncertainty, not creativity.

But when learners know the boundaries – what's expected, what's safe, what's allowed – they *relax*. They step in more fully. They contribute more courageously. They stretch further.

Because structure isn't limitation – it's liberation.

Your job is to create containers that hold the weight of deep, transformative interaction, without putting the emotional burden of figuring it out on your learners. When that's in place, they're not wasting energy trying to navigate ambiguity. They're using their energy to learn, apply, and grow.

The difference between activity and progress

It's easy to confuse busy sessions with effective ones.

But just because learners are talking doesn't mean they're moving.

Collaboration that drives transformation isn't just noisy. It's *aimed*. It's built on shared outcomes. It's focused, intentional, and infused with purpose.

If a peer review session doesn't include a prompt, a purpose, and a next step – it's just feedback theater. If a group sprint doesn't tie into a meaningful milestone – it's just collective chaos.

As the architect of your hybrid program, your role is to design collaboration that's not just interactive, but instrumental. It must move people forward. Clarify their thinking. Strengthen their skills. Build their confidence.

That doesn't require complexity. It requires care. Careful sequencing. Clear framing. Cultural leadership.

The stuff your learners won't even consciously notice – but will feel in every interaction. And when they feel it, they'll trust the process. They'll trust the group. And they'll trust themselves to lean in.

The signatures of a well-designed collaborative experience

Here's how you know your collaborative formats are working:

- People don't just participate. They *progress*.
- They finish sessions lighter, clearer, more confident.
- They move forward between calls – not because you assigned a task, but because they're internally compelled.
- They show up for each other – not out of obligation, but out of mutual investment.

They say things like:

- 'I've never shared that out loud before.'
- 'I didn't realise I was that close to a breakthrough.'
- 'This would've taken me months to figure out alone.'

That's when you know your design is working.

You've created a structure that holds without constraining.

You've designed collaboration without chaos.

You've built the bridge from connection to implementation.

And in doing so, you've unlocked something most programs never reach. A culture where doing the work together isn't an exception – it's the norm.

WHAT'S NEXT?

Collaboration accelerates learning. But it still needs a steady hand and a human presence to drive transformation forward.

In the next part, we explore the fourth pillar of the Hybrid Authority Formula: **coaching** – not as being always-on, but as intentional support that moves learners forward without draining you in the process.

Part V

COACHING: TURN YOUR PRESENCE INTO A MULTIPLIER

"

Coaching is the bridge that connects untapped potential to extraordinary achievements.

Maxime Lagacé[8]

"

This section explores coaching not as a drain on your time, but as a **strategic accelerant** – the high-leverage human layer that unlocks transformation.

You'll learn how to structure coaching inside a hybrid program so it's **effective, energizing, and scalable**.

This is where your presence becomes a multiplier, not a dependency.

13

Coaching that clicks

There's a moment that happens in every great learning journey. It's not when the learner finishes a module. It's not when they post in the group or tick off an action on their to-do list. It's when they finally see themselves differently. When they realize they're capable of more than they thought. When they shift from uncertainty to clarity, and from passively consuming knowledge to actively becoming the person who implements it.

That moment is rarely delivered by content alone. It doesn't come from a clever framework or a fancy platform. It comes from a human interaction. A reflection. A nudge. A question that lands at just the right time. That moment – the one that makes the rest of the program click into place – is almost always created through coaching.

This is the human edge. And it's what makes the coaching pillar of the Hybrid Authority Formula essential. Not optional.

In a world of asynchronous courses and automated funnels, coaching remains the most direct path to real transformation. But not just any coaching. We're not talking about endless Zoom calls or being on call for clients 24/7. We're talking about intentional, high-leverage, well-structured coaching moments that help learners think better, act faster, and move through resistance with clarity and confidence.

If the content pillar is about building your digital twin and the collaboration pillar is about getting learners into action with each other, the coaching pillar is where they get into alignment with themselves. It's where they're witnessed. Where they're challenged. Where they're supported through the emotional wobble that happens between idea and execution.

Why coaching is a strategic accelerant

Most learners don't fail because they didn't get enough information. They fail because they got stuck, and no one noticed. No one helped them process what they were experiencing. No one pulled them out of their spiral of second-guessing. No one asked the hard questions or named the thing they were too close to see.

Content alone can't do that. Community helps, but peer support has its limits. Collaboration keeps momentum going, but it's rarely tailored. The moment someone gets stuck in their own head, it takes a coach to help them out.

The more self-paced your program is, the more critical coaching becomes. Because when learners are on their own, the stakes of getting silently stuck are much higher. No one sees the tab that's been open for six weeks without action. No one hears the internal monologue that's sabotaging progress. No one knows they're about to quit – until they do.

That's where coaching steps in. Not to hold their hand or coddle them – but to intervene at the right time with the right question, and reorient them to what matters.

Think about the programs you've invested in yourself. Chances are, the ones that truly shifted you weren't just beautifully designed or packed with insight. They were the ones where someone helped you untangle the mess in your mind. Someone didn't just show you what to do – they showed you how to think differently.

That's the power of coaching. It's not about being the hero of your learners' journey. It's about being the mirror, the guide, the challenger, and the catalyst. And when delivered intentionally, even just a little coaching can unlock massive results.

The myth of 'unlimited access'

One of the biggest misconceptions in expert education is that coaching equals unlimited access: to be seen as valuable, you have to offer weekly calls, an always-monitored inbox, and constant availability.

But that model is not only unsustainable – it's ineffective.

More access does not equal more transformation. In fact, when coaching is always available, it loses its potency. It becomes background noise. Learners don't prepare as deeply, they don't reflect as thoroughly, and they don't value the interaction as much. Just like any scarce resource, the value of coaching increases when it's delivered deliberately.

In the Hybrid Authority Formula, coaching isn't about frequency – it's about precision. It's about inserting the right coaching moment at the right point in the learner journey. Maybe that's a decision-making checkpoint. Maybe it's after they submit their first implementation attempt. Maybe it's when they hit a known resistance pattern and need support reframing.

The point is, you don't have to coach all the time to be a great coach. You must coach when it matters. And you must do it in a way that aligns with your capacity and preserves your energy, so you can continue showing up with insight, not obligation.

From access to impact

Let's shift the conversation from access to impact.

The question is no longer, 'How much coaching do I include?'

It's, 'How do I design coaching moments that matter?'

Coaching inside a hybrid program isn't about building more calls into your calendar. It's about creating an intentional rhythm where support is available at key inflection points. Think of it as an opportunity for learners to gain clarity, recalibrate their focus, and re-engage with the work in front of them.

Sometimes that turning point happens in a one-off hot seat. Sometimes it's a check-in message or a 20-minute review that shifts their whole strategy. Sometimes it's a direct challenge: 'What are you avoiding right now?' That single question can do more than a two-hour workshop if it lands at the right moment.

Coaching is not about having all the answers. It's about helping the learner find *their* answers. It's about creating space for reflection, inviting insight, and guiding someone back to their own resourcefulness. When done well, coaching builds independence, not dependence.

It's not your job to walk them across the finish line. It's your job to make sure they don't forget why they started.

The emotional landscape of learning

Every learner brings more than just goals into a program. They bring baggage. Stories. Beliefs. Patterns. That emotional layer of learning is often the most unpredictable – and the most powerful.

And this is where coaching becomes irreplaceable.

Even the best content can't predict how someone will respond when things get hard. It can't tell when someone's self-doubt has hijacked their decision-making. It can't pause and say, 'Hey, I noticed something in your tone – what's really going on here?'

That level of insight only comes from human connection. And it's often the key to moving someone from stuck to unstuck.

Whether they're navigating imposter syndrome, perfectionism, fear of visibility, or plain old procrastination, coaching provides a safe container to bring those invisible blockers into the light. It doesn't solve everything. But it uncovers the friction – and that's often enough to start moving again.

In many ways, coaching is the emotional scaffolding of your program. It holds learners steady as they implement. It catches them when they wobble. It reminds them that what they're feeling is normal, but not a reason to quit.

Without this pillar, you risk creating an environment where learners intellectually agree with your content, but don't trust themselves enough to act on it.

The difference between teaching and coaching

The distinction between teaching and coaching is subtle but vital.

Teaching is about transferring knowledge. Coaching is about evoking growth.

As a teacher, you explain concepts, break down frameworks, and guide learners through a path of understanding. As a coach, you ask, 'What's getting in the way of applying this?' and then help the learner unpack their answer.

In a hybrid program, you will often wear both hats – but they require different postures. One is about expertise. The other is about presence.

When you coach, you're not performing. You're not broadcasting information. You're holding space, listening closely, and choosing your interventions with care. The magic is in the nuance.

Sometimes you need to slow the learner down. Sometimes you need to speed them up. Sometimes you just need to help them hear themselves more clearly.

Great coaching isn't about brilliance – it's about intentionality. And when paired with strong content and a rich community, it becomes the force multiplier that makes everything else stick.

Coaching doesn't have to be complicated

One of the most freeing realizations about coaching in the Hybrid Authority Formula is: it doesn't have to be formal, scheduled, or even face-to-face to be effective.

A 10-minute Loom reply can be coaching.

A written reflection prompt with tailored feedback can be coaching.

A simple question in a private thread – 'What feels hard right now?' – can be coaching.

What matters is that it's personal, timely, and connected to the learner's journey. It's about responding to the person, not just the progress report. And the more you can design your program to surface those moments naturally, the more lightweight coaching becomes.

This doesn't mean abandoning longer sessions or deeper conversations. It means expanding your definition of what coaching can look like – so you're not trapped in a binary of 'weekly calls or nothing.'

Coaching is where the work gets personal

At its core, coaching is the space where learning becomes personalized. It's where learners are no longer abstract avatars in your system, but real people with real needs.

It's where someone goes from 'I understand the concept' to 'I can see how this applies to me.'

It's where someone finally stops spinning and starts implementing.

It's where someone chooses to believe they're capable – and keeps going, even when it's hard.

That shift doesn't happen in isolation. It happens in a relationship. And that's why coaching isn't an afterthought in the Hybrid Authority Formula. It's a pillar.

Without it, you're left with well-packaged information and some group activity. With it, you're delivering transformation.

So, if you're building a hybrid learning experience that aims to truly move people, don't relegate coaching to an 'add-on.' Design it in. Structure it intentionally. Protect your time, yes – but protect the power of coaching even more.

Because when done well, coaching is the most human, the most irreplaceable, and the most transformational part of your entire program.

And in a world full of noise, that human edge is your advantage.

14

Coaching for momentum

Let's consider what keeps someone moving.

It's not motivation. That's fleeting. It shows up in short bursts – when a learner first joins your program, when they watch a particularly inspiring module, or when they attend a live session that leaves them buzzing. But motivation fades. Every learner, no matter how driven they seem on day one, will eventually hit a dip.

And when they do, what determines whether they keep going isn't willpower. It's structure. Specifically, a structure that includes the right type of coaching support – enough to help them recalibrate and refocus, but not so much that your business starts to depend on your constant presence.

This is where most experts struggle. Because they know coaching creates breakthroughs. They love it. They're good at it. But they also feel trapped by it. They've built programs that rely on them being in the room constantly, holding space, reacting to whatever a client throws their way. And while it might work for a few clients, it doesn't scale. It burns out the coach. It makes them the bottleneck. And ironically, it doesn't help the learner build independence.

So how do we design coaching in a way that fuels progress *and* sustainability? How do we create a model where learners feel supported, seen, and guided – but without you having to coach your way through every module, every block, every week?

It starts with understanding what *effective* coaching really looks like inside a hybrid program. And it continues with designing personalized touchpoints that serve as momentum multipliers – not dependency loops.

Let's start by reframing the role of coaching in your experience ecosystem.

Coaching as a catalyst, not a crutch

In many traditional models, coaching gets positioned as a service add-on. A bonus. 'You'll get X hours of support with me.' The underlying assumption is that the more coaching someone gets, the more valuable the program must be.

But here's the problem: when coaching is treated as a crutch, learners become passive. They wait to be told what to do next. They defer their decisions. They externalize responsibility. Coaching, instead of being a space for insight and clarity, becomes a catch-all for every hesitation and question.

That's not what we're building here.

Inside the Hybrid Authority Formula, coaching is a *designed* intervention. It's embedded not to hold learners up indefinitely, but to help them reconnect with their own clarity and move forward faster. It's not the handrail they cling to – it's the launchpad they push off from.

That's why we don't just coach for knowledge. We coach for momentum.

Momentum coaching is focused. Timed. Strategic. It's about helping learners move through known sticking points, take ownership of their progress, and build trust in their own capacity to act.

The goal isn't to give them all the answers. It's to help them ask better questions – and to know when to ask for help, and when to trust themselves to figure it out.

When you get this right, coaching becomes lighter. Cleaner. And *more powerful* – because you're no longer trying to carry the learner through the journey. You're helping them become the kind of person who finishes the journey themselves.

Designing for decision points

One of the simplest but most effective shifts you can make is to anchor your coaching around *decision points* – those natural moments in a learner's journey where they need to choose a direction, confirm understanding, or course-correct.

These aren't just checkpoints. They're points of potential divergence. Left unsupported, the learner might stall, overthink, or drift. But with a well-timed coaching touchpoint, you can help them move through the fog and back into focused, confident action.

A coaching touchpoint might come after they've completed your foundational content and need to clarify how they'll apply it in their own context. It might come after they've attempted their first implementation and are doubting whether they did it 'right.' It might appear mid-program when they're juggling competing priorities, starting to lose momentum, and need to realign with their original goals.

You don't need dozens of these moments. You just need to choose the *right ones* – the moments that statistically and emotionally matter most. When you design coaching around decision points, it stops being reactive and starts being predictive. You're not waiting for someone to get lost. You're showing up exactly where you know they're likely to wobble, and helping them stabilize.

This is the kind of coaching that makes your learners feel deeply supported, even if you're only interacting with them directly a handful of times.

Clarity, calibration, confidence

At its most powerful, coaching delivers three things: clarity, calibration, and confidence.

Clarity helps learners cut through the noise. When someone is overwhelmed or stuck, it's usually because they're trying to hold too many ideas in their head at once. Coaching strips away the clutter and gets to the core. What are you really trying to do here? What's the next right step? What matters most right now?

Calibration is about alignment. It's helping the learner compare where they think they are to where they are, and adjust accordingly. This might involve reviewing their plan, evaluating their results, or assessing the gap between intention and execution. It's where your expertise shines, because you can help them see things they've missed or refine their approach based on your bigger-picture view.

Confidence is the emotional payoff. It's the sense that 'I've got this.' Not because everything is perfect, but because they've been seen, guided, and encouraged at the right time. When someone walks away from a coaching session feeling clearer and more capable, you've done your job.

These three Cs are what coaching moments are for inside a hybrid program. They're what your learners need most – not endless cheerleading or weekly handholding. And they're what keep momentum alive, even when things get messy.

Building structure without being the structure

One of the hardest parts about transitioning from live delivery to a hybrid model is learning how to let go of constant presence. When you're accustomed to running workshops or weekly calls, it can feel unsettling to step back and let the structure support the learner instead.

But that's exactly what the Hybrid Authority Formula is designed to do. The structure *is* the support.

This doesn't mean removing yourself entirely. It means being strategic about where you place yourself. Your job is not to be the structure – it's to design the structure so that it reflects your coaching philosophy and supports the learner without requiring your presence at every step.

This might mean setting up defined coaching pathways: 'Once you reach this point, book your coaching check-in.' Or using self-assessment prompts to trigger reflection and signal when coaching might be needed: 'If you answered mostly B's, schedule a momentum call to recalibrate.'

When you build these flows into your program from the start, you create a sense of responsiveness without reaction. The learner knows where to go, what to do, and when to reach out. And you're not left playing inbox whack-a-mole every day.

This is how coaching becomes scalable – not because it disappears, but because it's framed inside a system that protects both the learner's progress and your energy.

Teaching people how to be coached

Here's an overlooked truth in program design: most learners don't naturally know how to be coached.

They don't know what a good question looks like. They don't know how to reflect before they show up. They don't know how to articulate what they need – especially when they're emotional, overwhelmed, or stuck in perfectionism.

If you don't set the tone, you'll end up with learners either not asking for help when they need it or flooding you with noise that doesn't lead anywhere.

That's why part of the coaching pillar is 'teaching people how to be coached.' Set expectations early. Model what a great coaching exchange looks like. Give them prompts or prep forms that guide their thinking. Ask them to reflect before they request. Encourage them to bring decisions, not just dilemmas.

You're not making them do more work. You're showing them how to make better use of the time and support you offer. And that, in turn, makes coaching more effective, more focused, and more impactful for both of you.

When learners learn how to be coached, they stop expecting you to solve their problems and start partnering with you to create solutions.

Your program, not your presence

Here's what it all comes down to: you don't need to be available constantly to create transformational results.

What you need is to design a program that does the heavy lifting – so that when you '*do*' show up, it matters. So that coaching is a spotlight, not a floodlight. So that your energy is preserved, your learners feel supported, and your program continues to deliver value whether you're online or off.

Coaching for momentum is not about doing more. It's about doing less, better. And trusting that your intentionally built hybrid structure will do what it's meant to: keep learners in motion, even when you're not in the room.

This is the evolution of coaching. Not less personal. Just more precise. Not more frequent. Just more focused.

And as you embrace this shift, you'll not only protect your capacity – you'll amplify your impact. Because when you stop tying progress to presence, you finally unlock the freedom to coach with power, not pressure.

15

Providing support without burnout

There's a moment every expert hits when their program is going well, their clients are engaged, and the outcomes are strong – but behind the scenes, they're fraying at the edges.

They're answering messages late at night. Rescheduling sessions around life. Quietly dreading their calendar. Feeling a pang of guilt every time a learner posts, 'Hey, quick question ... ' because the mental load of one more response feels like a landslide.

It doesn't start that way, of course. In the beginning, there's excitement. Gratitude. The thrill of being able to help someone one-on-one, to witness their growth, to walk beside them as they implement what you've created. But over time, if the structure isn't right – and if your boundaries aren't strong – coaching becomes a trap.

The very thing that made your program powerful starts draining your capacity.

And here's the harsh truth: no matter how effective your coaching is, if it depends on you being perpetually available, it won't last. Not for you. Not for your learners. Not for the mission you built this business to achieve.

This chapter is about solving that. It's about redefining the role you play inside your program, so you can protect your time, your energy, and your longevity. It's about replacing guilt with clarity. Obligation with design. And burnout with boundaries.

It's about building a coaching presence that's strong, impactful, and – most importantly – sustainable.

A boundary isn't a barrier

One of the most pervasive myths in the coaching world is that boundaries are cold. That limiting access equals limiting value. That saying no means you're not committed enough.

But let's turn that on its head.

What if the boundary isn't a barrier – but a container?

What if it's the boundary that creates the safety, structure, and focus that makes coaching possible in the first place?

A great coaching experience doesn't require unlimited access. In fact, unlimited access often creates more noise than clarity. It dilutes the intention behind each interaction. Learners show up unprepared, unclear, uncommitted – not because they're lazy, but because the container hasn't asked more of them.

When you set clear, kind, and well-communicated boundaries around how and when coaching happens, you don't diminish the experience. You elevate it. You signal that coaching is a space of value, not venting. That your time is precious – and so is theirs.

Boundaries are not walls. They're scaffolding. They hold everything up when the winds blow strong. And in a hybrid model – where so much of the delivery happens without you – your boundaries are part of the architecture that makes the whole thing work.

Coaching without becoming the bottleneck

Sustainability isn't just about energy. It's about design. And too often, experts build coaching into their programs like it's a vending machine: insert question, get instant response. Insert time, get access.

But here's the better model: coaching as a catalyst, not a conveyor belt.

Your goal isn't to be the person who answers every question. It's to be the person who helps learners ask better questions. The kind that move them forward. The kind that unlock decision-making, action, and ownership.

That's where coaching becomes leverage, not labor.

To get there, you need to stop being the default support structure – and start being the intentional touchpoint. That means having systems that hold the day-to-day questions. Clear channels that direct learners to the right resources before they turn to you. Group rhythms that allow them to self-regulate and self-correct.

It also means knowing when *not* to coach. Not every issue requires your intervention. Not every stuck moment is yours to solve. Sometimes, the most powerful coaching move is to say, 'This sounds like a conversation for your implementation group.' Or, 'Rewatch module four – your answer is already there.'

That's not dismissal. It's direction. And it teaches your learners to become more resilient, more resourceful, and more responsible for their own experience.

When you stop making yourself the solution to every problem, your coaching becomes stronger. Not weaker. Because now, when you do show up, it's meaningful. It's focused. And it's not just another notification to swipe away.

Stop over-giving; start over-designing

There's a sneaky pattern that shows up in a lot of programs led by heart-centered experts. It goes like this:

A learner hits a rough patch. They reach out. You care deeply about their success. You want to help. So you bend a little. Give them a bonus session. Reply to the late-night email. Make an exception. And another. And another.

Before long, your program becomes a patchwork of personal exceptions. And while your learners may be grateful in the short term, what they're experiencing is a version of your offer that only works because you're overextending yourself to hold it together.

That's not sustainable. And it's not scalable.

The real solution here isn't to give less. It's to design better.

Design coaching that's intentional. Predictable. Built into the program in ways that are visible, structured, and constrained in the best way.

That might look like milestone coaching – where learners unlock a 1:1 check-in after hitting specific markers. It might look like 'Office Hour' sessions, where access is live but limited. It might be through booking windows, calendar boundaries, or intake forms that ask, 'What have you already tried?' before they request help.

These aren't barriers. They're signals. They help learners show up more prepared, and they help you show up more powerfully.

When you over-give, you rescue. When you over-design, you equip. Choose the latter.

Detaching your worth from their wins

Let's talk about one of the most emotionally exhausting dynamics in coaching: tying your self-worth to your clients' results.

It's subtle, but pervasive.

They struggle, and you feel like you've failed them. They succeed, and you feel validated. Their pace, their progress, their mood – suddenly, it all feels like a reflection of you.

This mindset is toxic. Not just for you, but for them. Because it creates an invisible pressure. Your clients start to feel like they must perform for you. You start to feel like you must rescue them. And the whole relationship starts revolving around your need to be the hero.

That's not coaching. That's co-dependence.

Sustainable coaching requires emotional separation. Not detachment – but differentiation. You are not responsible for someone else's transformation. You are responsible for creating the conditions in which transformation can happen.

Their progress is theirs. Your presence is yours. Hold both with clarity and care.

You don't have to fix them. You don't have to carry them. You just must meet them in the moment, offer what's true, and trust that what you've built – the content, the community, the structure – is doing its job.

Your job is not to hold the whole thing together. It's to hold your role, fully and faithfully.

From exhausted expert to empowered authority

Coaching can be the most fulfilling part of your work. But only when it's shaped around your capacity, your values, and your business model – not your guilt.

When you build your hybrid program with this in mind, coaching becomes energizing again. It becomes a space of alignment, insight, and real-time transformation – not a never-ending drain on your time.

You get to be generous without being overrun. You get to be personal without being always-on. You get to build something that scales, not because you disappear – but because you've designed it that way.

You didn't build your program to become a service provider again. You built it to lead. To teach. To spark change. And you can't do that from the bottom of your own inbox.

So reclaim your boundaries. Rethink your rhythms. Build a coaching model that's as brave as it is sustainable.

Because if you want your program to last, your energy must last with it.

And when you honor that, your coaching doesn't get smaller – it gets sharper. It becomes a force that fuels your learners and your mission, not one that drains you.

This is the future of coaching in hybrid learning.

Intentional. Empowering. Built to last.

WHAT'S NEXT?

You've explored each of the four pillars: content, community, collaboration, and coaching.

Now it's time to bring them together.

In the next part, we shift from understanding to 'architecture' – laying out the structure, sequence, and core components of your hybrid experience.

PART VI

DESIGNING YOUR HYBRID EXPERIENCE

"

Blended learning has the potential
to transform education by personalizing
learning experiences and leveraging
the power of technology.

Arne Duncan[9]

"

---

[9] Arne Duncan is a former US Secretary of Education known for advocating
technology-driven, personalized approaches to learning.

This is where we bring everything together. You'll walk through a clear, structured method to design a Hybrid Authority Experience from the ground up:

1. Define the prize.
2. Create the offer.
3. Build the assets.
4. Activate access.

This is the blueprint phase – where theory turns into architecture.

16

From theory to program

Until now, we've been laying the foundation. You've explored why digital learning alone isn't enough. You've seen the cracks in conventional content-driven courses. And now, you're ready to build something different – something better.

This chapter marks the beginning of that shift.

From here forward, we move into the practical process of **designing your hybrid program** – not as a collection of course materials, but as a cohesive, transformational experience.

And to do that, we'll follow the **Hybrid Authority Formula**.

The Hybrid Authority Formula: your delivery blueprint

The Hybrid Authority Formula isn't about marketing, funnels, or filling your program. It's not about how people find you. This part of the journey is about what happens *after they join*. It's about designing the experience they'll move through – the structure that supports their transformation.

It gives you a system for building a learning experience that works – because it blends structured content, meaningful connection, collaborative momentum, and personalized support.

It's the answer to:

- How do I deliver on the promise my program makes?
- How do I deliver transformation at scale?
- How do I build assets that support my learners without burning me out?
- How do I create something that people finish, implement, and rave about?

Let's walk through how it unfolds.

The four-stage hybrid creation process

Designing your hybrid program is a structured, step-by-step journey. And it doesn't start with tech platforms or filming content. It starts with **clarity of purpose**.

Here's the full creation process this section of the book will guide you through.

Stage 1: Define the prize

This is where you get crystal clear on who your program is for and what they want most. You'll identify their biggest pain points, articulate the transformation they're seeking, and map out the before-and-after journey your experience must deliver.

This is where relevance is built – and resonance begins.

Stage 2: Create the offer

Once the desired transformation is clear, you'll design the structure that delivers it. You'll outline your method, define the key outcomes, and determine the format and flow that makes the promise achievable.

This is about more than deliverables – it's about designing a coherent, compelling promise that your program is built to keep.

Stage 3: Build the assets

Now we shift into creation. This is where you build the assets and ecosystem that power your hybrid experience. This will include:

- **Content:** Clear, structured, self-paced resources that let learners move forward without waiting on you.
- **Community:** A space for connection, peer learning, and support that deepens engagement.
- **Collaboration:** Purposeful formats that get learners implementing together and learning through doing.
- **Coaching:** Thoughtfully designed support touchpoints that offer guidance, accountability, and personalization.

Each of these is built intentionally, not bolted on. They work together to create an ecosystem that moves people forward.

Stage 4: Activate the access

With your assets in place, it's time to bring the experience to life.

This means launching with intention, onboarding learners clearly, creating early momentum, and supporting sustained progress through rhythm, structure, and connection.

It's not about the technology or automation. It's about ensuring the first experience within your program makes them feel they've made the right choice.

What this section will do

In the chapters that follow, we'll walk through each of these four stages in depth. You'll learn how to:

- design a program your audience genuinely wants
- architect an offer that's clear and compelling
- build the assets that support transformation
- launch and deliver with confidence, clarity, and care.

This isn't about overwhelming your learners – or yourself. It's about creating a hybrid experience that delivers results and scales your impact without sacrificing connection.

Let's build your hybrid program – one powerful piece at a time.

17

Define the prize: ruthless relevance and real pain

You might think the most powerful programs begin with the curriculum. But the truth is, they begin with clarity. Not just clarity about what you want to teach. Clarity about who you're solving a problem for – and what that problem is in their world, not yours.

Before you design an experience, before you outline a single module, you need to decide: who is this really for? And what problem are they desperate to solve?

If you skip this step – if you race into content production or tech setup without anchoring your aim – you'll end up building something no one is urgently looking for. You'll launch with crickets. You'll second-guess your work. And you'll wonder if hybrid delivery is the problem.

It's not.

The real issue? You missed the starting line.

This chapter is about reclaiming that foundation. It's about building from ruthless relevance, not wishful thinking. And it starts with four critical steps that will shape everything else in your program – from the promise you make, to the format you deliver, to the way your learners show up and engage.

Let's walk through each one.

Step 1: Start with ruthless relevance

Relevance is not reach – it's recognition

This step is not about who you *could* help. It's about who you are *designing* for. That distinction matters more than most experts realize. Because relevance is not broad. It's specific. It's not about industry labels or ideal client avatars. It's about entering the real conversation happening in someone's mind.

Speak the language of lived experience

Relevance doesn't mean targeting 'female entrepreneurs' or 'corporate teams.' It means you've pinpointed a real, felt problem – and you're framing your offer in language that makes someone feel seen, sometimes for the first time. When that happens, you stop pushing your program. People start pulling themselves toward it.

Because when a learner sees themselves in your message, when they feel like you get them, they trust you can guide them. That trust is what fuels enrolment. That trust is what drives engagement. And that trust is what creates transformation.

The fear of niching – and the case for choosing a lane

If you feel resistance here, you're not alone. Most experts do. You might be thinking, 'I can help so many different people,' or, 'I don't want to niche down too far,' or, 'My method works across industries.' And all of that might be true. But here's the harder truth: a program that's for everyone rarely works for anyone.

Because when you try to appeal to everyone, you dilute the very thing that makes your experience powerful – your deep insight into a specific problem. Relevance requires focus. So the invitation is simple: choose a lane. Not forever. Just for this offer. Pick one ideal learner. One urgent problem. One compelling outcome.

This is where transformation begins.

Step 2: Pinpoint the pain they already feel

Pain comes first – even if you wish it didn't

This is the emotional heartbeat of your offer – and it's where most experts misstep. They want to jump to solutions. To showcase the method. To lead with logic.

Let's be honest – most experts don't want to talk about pain. They want to talk about their solution. Their method. Their frameworks. Their brilliance. But people don't buy brilliance. They buy relevance. They buy relief.

You're not diagnosing – you're describing

They don't walk around looking for your system. They walk around trying to fix something that's bothering them. The moment they see something that promises relief, they respond.

That's why we start here. Before we design an experience. Before we create an offer. Before we layer in content or community or coaching. We must first answer a single, powerful question: what's keeping your ideal learner stuck?

And not from your perspective. From theirs.

Not what you've diagnosed as the root cause. Not what you think they need to understand better. But the thing they're struggling with right now – the part they're Googling late at night, the silent frustration they carry around all day, the point where they're ready to say, 'I can't keep doing it this way.'

Pain opens the door; your offer is a bridge

The most powerful hybrid programs aren't built around your expertise. They're built around your learner's exhaustion. Not the deep, systemic issue you've mapped out – but the version of the problem they can already name.

Behind every enrolment is a moment of breakdown. They didn't join because your curriculum is well-structured. They joined because they're sick of second-guessing themselves. Because they're overwhelmed, underpaid, or under-fulfilled – and ready for that to change.

People don't want to buy a drill bit. They want a hole.

They're looking for an outcome. For clarity. For momentum. So when your message starts by naming the thing they're struggling with – and framing your experience as the natural next step – you're not competing with other programs. You're becoming the only one that makes sense.

Pain opens the door. Once someone walks through it, your job is to build a bridge. That bridge connects where they are now to where they want to be. And that bridge needs to be solid. Clear. Believable. That's what your hybrid program becomes. But it all starts here – with the pain that opens the door.

Step 3: Identify the prize they actually want

People don't want learning – they want the shift

Every great hybrid program offers a prize. A clear and compelling end state. A shift. A before-and-after that matters deeply to the learner. And the prize is not your content. It's not your process. It's the tangible transformation someone walks away with. The new behavior they can confidently execute. The problem they no longer have. The way they now see themselves differently.

When you define the prize, you define the purpose of everything that follows. Not just in terms of design, but in how your program is positioned, how your learners show up, and how they measure their own success.

The Three-Lens Clarity Map

To uncover that prize, we step out of expert mode and into empathy. The Three-Lens Clarity Map helps you stop designing for what you want to teach and start designing for what your learners need to solve:

- **The Human Lens** asks who your learner is as a person – what they value, fear, dream of, and feel stuck between.
- **The Problem Lens** surfaces what they're struggling with day-to-day, what they've tried and failed, and what that problem is costing them emotionally, financially, and reputationally.
- **The Progress Lens** defines what success looks like to them – not in theory, but in concrete, meaningful results they'd pay to achieve.

When you map all three lenses, something clicks. You're no longer guessing what your offer should promise. You're building it around what your learner is already hoping for, sometimes without even realizing it.

You're stepping into their story, walking beside them, and offering a way forward that feels natural and grounded.

Step 4: Distil it into an impact statement

Build your entire experience around one clear outcome

Once you've clarified who your program is for, what they're trying to escape, and where they want to go, you're ready to distil it into one clear sentence: the impact statement.

This isn't just a clever positioning line. It's the distilled essence of your hybrid program – the transformation it promises, anchored in ruthless relevance. Once written, this sentence becomes the north star for everything that follows: your delivery, your messaging, your onboarding, your sales page, your learner journey.

The impact statement template

Before anyone cares how your program works, they need to know what it *does*. That's where the impact statement comes in:

> 'This program helps [ideal client] [transformation], achieving [measurable result], without [pain], so they can [meaningful outcome].'

Here are some examples:

> 'This program helps mid-level managers lead high-impact strategic conversations, earning recognition and influence in leadership settings – without being dismissed or talked over – so they can contribute meaningfully to business direction.'

'This experience helps freelance designers build a magnetic personal brand that attracts premium, high-paying clients consistently – without relying on referrals or content burnout – so they can increase income and design on their terms.'

'This program helps course creators package their IP into a leveraged hybrid offer that consistently delivers client results and scalable income – without working around the clock or managing endless tech – so they can grow sustainably and reclaim their time.'

Notice what's *not* in these statements. No mention of content. No talk of modules. No frameworks or features. Just pain, person, and progress.

That's the prize.

A moment of clarity you can build everything around

So here's the invitation: take 10 minutes. No fluff. No jargon. Just get honest. Who is this really for? What are they stuck on right now? What does success look like from their view?

Then write it:

'This program helps [ideal client] [transformation], achieving [measurable result], without [pain], so they can [meaningful outcome].'

When you can do that, you have something worth building. Something worth enrolling in. Something worth scaling. Because you're no longer designing from expert bias – you're designing from learner urgency.

You've defined the prize. Now it's time to build the offer that delivers it.

Apply what you've clarified

This chapter laid the strategic foundation for everything that follows. But clarity isn't just a shift in mindset – it's something you need to **capture, refine, and commit to.**

Before you move on, finalize the following:

1. **Choose your learner lane.** Define who this program is really for. Be specific. One ideal learner. One urgent problem. One outcome they truly want.

2. **Write out their real pain.** Describe the frustration, fear, or friction they're experiencing – in their words, not yours. What would they say to a friend? What are they secretly sick of dealing with?

3. **Complete the Three-Lens Clarity Map.** Use the Human, Problem, and Progress Lenses to step into your learner's world. Write down what they value, what they're stuck on, and what success looks like to *them.*

4. **Craft your impact statement.** Use the formula: 'This program helps [ideal client] [transformation], achieving [measurable result], without [pain], so they can [meaningful outcome].' This is the transformation your entire program will deliver. Make it specific. Make it powerful. Make it true.

These four elements are not optional – they are the bedrock of relevance, enrolment, and results.

Lock them in.

Because in the next chapter, you'll turn this clarity into a structured, sellable offer.

18

Create the offer: build a path not just a product

A powerful program doesn't start with a curriculum. It starts with a clear, structured offer that delivers on a specific promise.

That's your job now.

You've already clarified the transformation your learner is seeking. What you're doing in this chapter is engineering the path that gets them there, and packaging that path into a product you can sell and deliver with confidence.

This isn't about stacking modules or listing deliverables. It's about **designing a structured experience** that solves a real problem in a defined way, with a format that supports implementation and drives results.

This is where your offer becomes more than an idea. It becomes a *product*.

Let's get to work.

Step 1: Map the milestones of transformation

Creating a transformational offer doesn't start with content. It starts with clarity, and then works backwards.

Look at the outcome your program promises. What does success look like from the learner's perspective? What result have you committed to delivering?

Now reverse-engineer the journey that gets them there.

Start at the end. Then ask: what must happen – step by step – for someone to experience that transformation?

What do they need to understand, build, change, decide, or apply along the way?

This is where you shift from clarity to structure. Your job here is to map out the **three to seven critical milestones** that a learner must pass through on their way from problem to progress. These are not arbitrary 'modules.' These are **distinct stages of transformation** – each one a necessary and measurable shift.

You're not laying out content. You're engineering a results path.

From clear outcome to guided journey

You've already articulated the promise your program delivers: **'This program helps [specific person] solve [specific problem] so they can [specific result].'**

Now your job is to map the path that makes that promise real.

As a learning designer, you're building a guided experience that moves someone through predictable, progressive change. And that change doesn't happen all at once. It happens through structured shifts – moments of clarity, capability, and confidence that stack into transformation.

Each stage must focus on a specific outcome: a behavior change, a mindset shift, a skill gained, a bottleneck removed.

They are not abstract themes or vague content buckets. They must:

- solve a relevant, high-stakes problem at that point in the journey
- equip the learner with something they can do, use, or demonstrate
- be supported through all four elements of the Hybrid Authority Formula:
  - **content** to explain and model the shift
  - **coaching** to personalize and guide progress
  - **collaboration** to apply and integrate through shared effort
  - **community** to normalize the experience and sustain momentum.

This is where your program becomes more than information – it becomes an engine for progress. Each stage isn't just something to learn. It's something to accomplish.

Structure with intentionality

Let's be clear: you're not designing a 12-week 'info dump.' You're building a transformational journey. So don't default to generic structures like 'Week 1: Introduction / Week 2: Core Concepts.' That's not how real progress happens – and it's not what your learner is signing up for.

You're not creating an academic syllabus. You're designing a journey of results.

Ask yourself:

- What needs to happen first to create early traction?

- Where will they hit natural resistance, and how can you anticipate that?
- What's the emotional rhythm of the program – clarity, momentum, doubt, breakthrough?
- How can each stage build belief, competence, and follow-through?

When you structure around real transformation – not convenience or habit – you build something that earns attention, respect, and results.

Write each milestone as a shift: 'At this point in the journey, my learner will have [built, solved, implemented, learned, decided …].' If you can't finish that sentence with precision, you're not ready to move on.

Once these stages are set, you'll have the spine of your offer. What comes next is filling those stages with intentional, outcome-driven action.

Step 2: Define the work inside each milestone

You've already committed to ruthless relevance. Now it's time to bring that clarity into the structure. For each milestone, map what your learner must do – and then strip away anything that doesn't support that motion. If a lesson, template, or activity doesn't help your learner progress, it doesn't belong. This step isn't about content delivery. It's about enabling forward movement.

Zoom in on the journey

What is it your learner needs to be able to do to complete this milestone? What are the real-world actions, tasks, or decisions that represent success here? And what specific activities, support, or challenges will help them do that?

Design for action, not information

Underneath those actions, what essential knowledge must they have? What do they need to understand or believe to perform those actions effectively and confidently? This knowledge must be ruthlessly relevant. If it doesn't directly support the actions needed to complete the milestone, it doesn't belong. The goal is to support, not swamp.

Remember, your learners are already busy and likely overwhelmed. Cognitive overload is a serious risk in any learning experience. When learners are hit with too much information, especially content that feels irrelevant or poorly timed, they disengage, lose motivation, and mentally check out. They stop connecting the dots. They start doubting their ability to succeed. And when the path forward feels heavy instead of clear, even high-potential learners begin to opt out – internally, if not yet externally.

Every single concept or piece of knowledge you include must earn its place. If it doesn't directly enable the learner to complete an action, decide, or achieve the milestone – it doesn't belong. Ruthless relevance is the filter here. Your job is not to impress. Your job is to equip. Equip them with just enough of the right knowledge to do the next thing, and nothing more.

Strip out the non-essentials

'What does the learner need to do, learn, and experience at each stage?' That is your test. Anything else is clutter. Maybe it's mapping out a new workflow. Making a pricing decision. Designing a plan. Creating an asset. Running a pilot. Making a pitch. Testing a tool. Shifting a belief.

Each milestone should contain a **learner-facing challenge or action** that proves progress. This is how you keep people engaged – not through volume, but through visible traction.

Define success criteria inside the milestone

Design from the learner's side. What are they capable of at the end of this stage that they weren't at the start? How do they know they're ready to move forward?

Define that. Then build backwards. Only include what they *need* to achieve that shift. Nothing else.

This is where you protect your offer from bloat. If it doesn't create progress, cut it. Your offer should be tight, intentional, and impossible to ignore.

What does success look like *inside* each milestone? Don't think in terms of content. Think in terms of output. What is the learner producing, solving, practicing, or completing? This is how transformation gets built – step by step, through applied action.

Step 3: Craft the impact statement

Now that your program is structured and the learner's journey is clear, it's time to turn that clarity into a sentence that sells the experience.

This is your anchor. A single line that distils the entire experience into something tangible, urgent, and unmistakably useful. It's not just a headline – it's the positioning core of your offer. It tells your prospective client exactly who the program is for, what it helps them overcome, and what result they can expect.

This statement doesn't just clarify the value. It sets the tone for how your program is perceived, packaged, and promoted.

It's what creates instant resonance – or misses the mark. That's why it must be sharp, specific, and emotionally true to your learner's reality.

Use a simple, specific formula

We covered the formula for this in the previous chapter.

The simplicity of the formula is its strength. No features. No fluff. No need to overexplain. Just a clear promise to solve something important and deliver something desired.

Put it to work

This is the line that lives everywhere – on your sales page, in your webinar pitch, at the top of your one-pager. It communicates value in 10 seconds or less. It's how people understand what they're buying – and why it matters.

Make it stick

This is how you make your offer repeatable, referable, and easy to remember. It gives people language they can repeat. It helps others sell it for you. And most importantly, it makes the value feel instantly obvious.

It's how your offer moves beyond your delivery – and begins to stand on its own.

Step 4: Design the flow of the hybrid experience

You've defined what your program delivers. You've mapped the journey and shaped each stage. Now you need to guide your learners through it – with rhythm, energy, and consistency. This is where you design the flow of the experience.

You're not deciding between 'live' or 'self-paced.' You're choreographing how people move from one stage to the next, with just the right mix of structure, support, and momentum to keep them progressing.

Build rhythm before you build a schedule

Most course creators jump straight to calendars. Eight weeks or twelve? One call per week or two? But sequence without rhythm is shallow. The real work is designing a learner experience that makes forward motion feel inevitable.

Start by asking: where does the energy dip? Where do people typically get stuck? What cadence of support builds trust without building dependency?

Design the rhythm of progress – then decide how it lands on the calendar.

Use the four pillars to drive progress

Flow is not about format. It's about the integration of the four core elements of hybrid delivery.

Content should be released deliberately. Whether you drip it weekly, gate it behind completion, or tie it to milestones – don't dump everything on day one. Content that's timed right keeps people focused.

Coaching needs rhythm. Whether weekly, milestone-triggered, or blended, learners need predictability. When support is structured – not scattered – it builds confidence and commitment.

Collaboration needs to be designed into the learning, not added later. Think shared challenges, peer reviews, and small breakout groups. These moments move people from theory to implementation.

Community needs to be alive, not passive. It's not a comment thread – it's the connective tissue between milestones. Celebrate wins, surface stuck points, and keep momentum visible.

Choose a flow structure that matches your model

One of the most important choices you'll make is whether your program follows a cohort model or what we'll call a rolling hybrid model.

In a **cohort-based model**, everyone starts together. There's a launch date, a shared arc, and a collective rhythm. Learners journey through the stages side by side. This model builds a strong sense of camaraderie. It supports emotionally demanding transformations. And it makes live elements like group coaching and collaboration feel electric. The downside? You need launch cycles, you can't accept learners any time, and you'll likely need to deliver more in real time.

In a rolling hybrid model, learners can join at any time. They move through the stages at their own pace. Content is self-paced, but the four pillars still apply – they just need to be systematized. You'll need automated onboarding. You'll need clear orientation pathways. And your coaching and collaboration may be milestone-triggered rather than calendar-based. This model is more scalable, but it takes stronger facilitation to maintain engagement.

Neither is better. Each has trade-offs. Your job is to choose the one that matches your learners, your delivery style, and your capacity.

Design for completion, not access

The best hybrid programs don't just provide access – they promote follow-through.

Flow that supports completion makes learners feel safe, seen, and in control. There's no confusion about what to do next. No empty gaps between milestones. No motivation lost to ambiguity.

Design a flow that builds belief at every stage. That creates momentum, not stress. That doesn't rely on pressure, but on progress.

When your learners feel the rhythm of movement and the consistency of support, they don't just stay – they finish. And that's when your offer delivers what it was designed to do.

Bring your offer into focus

You now have all the core components of a strategic, high-impact hybrid offer. But clarity without completion won't move your business forward, or change lives.

Before you move on to building the assets that deliver your offer, take time to finalize the following:

1. **Craft your offer statement:** Write the one-line promise that captures your program's purpose. Use the structure: 'This program helps [ideal client] [transformation], achieving [measurable result], without [pain], so they can [meaningful outcome].' It should be specific, outcome-focused, and easy for others to repeat.

2. **Define your three to seven milestones:** List the transformation checkpoints your learner will move through. Each one should reflect visible progress that builds belief and capability – stage by stage.

3. **Map the core work of each milestone:** For each stage, define what your learner will do, apply, or produce – and

what knowledge is truly essential to help them do it. Filter ruthlessly. Only keep what drives action.

4. **Design the flow:** Choose your rhythm and structure. Decide on pacing, access (cohort or rolling), timing of support, and how each of the four pillars – content, coaching, collaboration, and community – shows up throughout the journey.

These four decisions are not checkboxes. They are the foundation of a leveraged, learner-centered offer – one that's ready to build, deliver, and scale.

Once these four elements are finalized, you're ready to move into the next phase: turning your offer into delivery assets that bring it to life, stage by stage, with intention and impact.

19

Build the assets: what your learners really need

You've shaped the offer. You've designed the flow. Now it's time to build the assets that bring it all to life.

This is where your program becomes real – not just in your head, but in the hands of your learners. These are the materials, systems, and structures that make your hybrid experience deliverable, repeatable, and scalable.

You're not building content for the sake of it. You're building what's required to support progress at every stage. This isn't about volume – it's about velocity. You're constructing the pieces that move people forward.

Let's walk through how to do that with clarity, focus, and intention.

Step 1: Inventory what needs to be built

You've mapped your milestones. You've defined the flow. Now it's time to identify what assets must be created to turn those ideas into a living, breathing experience.

This step is about alignment. Not creativity. Not ideation. Alignment.

You're anchoring every asset you build to one purpose: learner progress. Not production value. Not platform bells and whistles. Just forward motion.

Start with the end in mind

Return to each milestone and ask: what is the learner supposed to be able to do at this stage? What decision, skill, action, or outcome needs to happen for them to progress?

From there, map backwards. For each milestone, identify what the learner needs to:

- understand clearly
- apply confidently
- navigate without confusion.

This tells you what to build – not what you want to create, but what your learner needs to succeed.

Map across the four pillars

Each milestone should include intentional support across the Hybrid Authority Formula model. Ask yourself:

- **Content:** What digital asset needs to be in place to explain or demonstrate the shift?
- **Coaching:** What kind of feedback, check-in, or live support is needed to prevent stalls?

- **Collaboration:** What peer interaction or shared activity deepens the application?
- **Community:** What kind of visibility, recognition, or encouragement sustains momentum?

Every asset you build must serve one purpose: forward motion. Not polish. Not platform preferences. Progress. You've already filtered what matters. Now, this step is about discipline – making sure what you build is aligned, necessary, and lean. If it doesn't move the learner forward, it doesn't belong.

Focus on the minimum effective build

You're not producing a content library. You're building a result-generating machine.

Each asset should earn its place. This is about effectiveness, not exhaustiveness. You're not aiming to impress – you're aiming to help.

Once your inventory is complete, you'll have a clear list of exactly what to build – and why.

What comes next is creating those assets with precision and purpose.

Step 2: Build the content that guides

Content is where your ideas become tools. Not lectures. Not theory. Tools that your learner can use to move forward.

Build around the action, not the topic

Every piece of content you create should start with the question: what do I want the learner to *do* after this?

Don't default to a lesson just because it fits a framework. Design the asset that helps someone take the next step toward the milestone. That might be:

- a written guide that explains a process or unpacks a core concept
- a short video – live action, animated, or screencast – that shows a key technique in motion
- an interactive learning element like a quiz, decision tree, or scenario simulation
- a checklist, worksheet, or template that enables immediate application.

The medium isn't the point. Clarity is. Choose the format that best helps the learner take meaningful action.

If the content isn't making action easier, clearer, or faster – it's filler.

Make your content your digital twin

Think of content as the version of you that scales. It should guide, explain, and model as well as you would live – but without you being there. That means:

- clear language, not clever phrasing
- one outcome per asset
- no unnecessary theory – just what helps unlock motion.

Chunk your content into digestible parts. If it's overwhelming, they won't start. If it's unclear, they won't finish. And if it's boring, they won't remember it.

Design it like you're handing them the keys to progress – not inviting them into an archive.

Build minimum effective versions first

You don't need a full studio. You need clarity.

Draft the scripts. Record the draft. Test it with one person. Ask: did this help you act?

If yes, it's enough. If no, refine it.

The goal is to help them move – not to get stuck building content you're too tired to finish or too embarrassed to share.

Content is not the star of the show. The learner is. Your content is just the lever that helps them move forward without you holding the weight.

Step 3: Set up the support systems

Support isn't just a safety net – it's a momentum engine. When done well, it keeps learners engaged, accountable, and in motion.

Make coaching predictable and purposeful

Coaching gives your learners access to perspective, feedback, and personalized problem-solving. But it only works when it's designed – not just offered.

Start by deciding what kind of coaching is right for your program:

- Live calls to deepen insight, celebrate wins, or work through blockers?
- Milestone-triggered feedback that's baked into the journey?
- Asynchronous voice notes or review threads that give support without delay?

Then set the rhythm. Weekly? Fortnightly? At the completion of each stage? Coaching works when learners know what to expect and when.

You don't need to be available 24/7. You just need to be reliable. Your coaching shouldn't feel like a lifeline – it should feel like part of the architecture.

Design collaboration that drives application

Collaboration isn't just social. It's strategic. It's what turns knowledge into skill.

Map out how learners will work together – and why it matters. That might include:

- peer review or critique cycles
- shared planning or implementation challenges
- small group masterminds or breakout sessions
- collaborative assets, builds, or co-created work.

Don't create interaction for the sake of it. Design collaboration that gives people a reason to show up and something meaningful to do when they get there.

Support systems don't just keep learners afloat. They push them forward. They close the gap between intention and action. When you design them with care, your program doesn't just run – it lifts.

Step 4: Design the community experience

Community isn't an optional extra. It's what turns your program from transactional to transformational.

When built with intention, it becomes the space where learners stay engaged between milestones, where they see themselves reflected in others, and where your culture does some of the heavy lifting for motivation.

Define the role the community plays

Start by clarifying the purpose. What is the community *for*?

- Is it a place for emotional support when doubt sets in?
- Is it where learners post wins to build momentum?
- Is it used for feedback, questions, or real-time accountability?

Be explicit. If the community's role isn't clear, it becomes background noise – or worse, a ghost town.

Design the rhythm of interaction

Next, give it structure. Communities need rhythm, not randomness. What regular moments will keep it alive?

- Weekly prompts or reflection threads?
- Check-ins to kick off the week?
- Celebration posts to close it?
- Monthly AMAs or casual drop-in sessions?

Design interaction patterns that keep people contributing, not just consuming. Don't wait for connection – engineer it.

Set the tone and culture

Finally, think about how it feels to be inside your space. What are the social norms? What's encouraged? What's not?

Is it supportive and celebratory? Quiet and thoughtful? Fast-paced and practical?

You set the tone from the start – through your onboarding, your facilitation style, and what you model.

When your community is designed to be active, safe, and purposeful, it doesn't just support your content. It elevates it.

It's not a chat thread. It's a shared experience. One that makes your program something learners *want* to come back to.

Make it real and ready

You've done the strategic thinking. You've mapped what matters. Now it's time to commit to action.

Before you move into the next stage of activation, complete these steps:

1. **Finalize your asset inventory.** Go back to each milestone and list the exact content, coaching, collaboration, and community elements needed. If it doesn't support the learner's next step, remove it.

2. **Draft your minimum viable content assets.** Create first-pass versions of the tools your learners will use. Videos, templates, guides, checklists – make them actionable, focused, and aligned to the outcome. Don't polish. Just produce.

3. **Design your coaching and collaboration cadence.** Lock in the rhythm of your support. When will coaching happen? What format will collaboration take? How will learners stay engaged with you and each other?

4. **Map the structure of your community.** Clarify its purpose. Set its rituals. Define how and when it will create visibility, motivation, and connection between learners.

When these four steps are complete, your offer becomes a real experience – not just an idea with potential.

Now, you're ready to activate access and bring learners into the journey.

20

Activate the access: onboarding that builds trust

You've built the offer. You've designed the delivery. Now it's time to bring people in.

This chapter is about what happens between 'yes, I'm in' and 'I'm on my way.' That critical window between sale and transformation, where trust is either cemented or cracked. Where momentum either begins or dies.

Great hybrid programs don't start with a module. They start with a moment.

And that moment needs to be clear, intentional, and energizing. How your learners enter your program sets the tone for everything that follows.

Let's walk through how to activate access in a way that creates confidence, builds connection, and kickstarts progress from day one.

Step 1: Design the entry point

The learner experience doesn't start when someone logs into your platform. It starts the moment they say yes. That moment is the threshold – and how you manage it determines whether they feel momentum or regret.

A clunky entry breeds doubt. A clean, intentional one builds belief.

Make the first moment count

That first touchpoint after someone joins isn't a formality. It's your first chance to deliver the feeling that matters most: *this was a smart decision.*

The welcome message, email, or video must reaffirm the transformation they're here for, normalize any uncertainty they're carrying, and give them instant confidence that they're in the right place. Don't default to a dry transaction. Don't send them a receipt and think your work is done.

Remove hurdles immediately

What happens next should feel like momentum, not mystery. A seamless access system is essential. That means immediate, jargon-free instructions, login links that work everywhere, and direct entry to a clearly marked first step – not a cluttered dashboard.

If someone joins and immediately hits a wall – because something doesn't work, isn't obvious, or feels overwhelming – you've lost critical energy. Smooth access creates momentum.

Anchor emotion, not just logistics

Most access flows deliver information. Great ones create emotion.

That early experience should generate a sense of clarity, excitement, and confidence. You want learners to think: this is already working. I'm excited to be here. I know what to do next.

If your entry point doesn't create those feelings, rewrite it. How they feel on day one determines how they show up for everything that follows.

Step 2: Build the onboarding experience

Onboarding isn't about orientation. It's about activation.

The job of onboarding is to convert curiosity into commitment. You're guiding your learner from 'I bought this' to 'I'm becoming someone new.' That doesn't happen with a few welcome screens.

Turn information into traction

Most onboarding dumps information: start here, click that, good luck.

Yours should build traction. That means every part of your onboarding experience should reinforce the value of the program, show learners how the journey works, and prompt an early sense of progress.

This might include a powerful welcome video to frame the journey and set expectations, a visual roadmap of the program's structure, and a clear walkthrough of where they'll experience content, coaching, collaboration, and community.

Engineer a win within 24 hours

Momentum starts when learners *do* something that makes them feel accomplished. Give them something they can act on immediately – whether that's introducing themselves, completing a short quiz, downloading a toolkit, or choosing their focus for the first milestone.

You're not just onboarding – they're onboarding themselves. Make that process intuitive, encouraging, and fast.

If they feel like they've made progress on day one, they'll believe they can keep going.

Step 3: Set the rhythm and expectations

Confusion kills progress. Ambiguity creates disengagement. The cure? Rhythm.

Rhythm isn't about structure for structure's sake – it's about creating safety. When people know what to expect, they show up with purpose.

Establish a beat that learners can follow

From the start, communicate exactly how the program flows. Let them know when content is released, when and how coaching is available, what engagement looks like in the community, and how feedback or reminders will support them throughout.

Don't assume people will figure it out. Spell it out. Repetition creates reliability, and reliability builds trust.

Set the cultural standard early

The first few days aren't just about logistics. They're about tone.

Make learners feel welcomed, seen, and energized. Highlight early wins. Encourage participation with light but intentional engagement. This is where you establish the values and behaviors that shape the experience moving forward.

Step 4: Create early momentum

You only get one shot at their first real win.

Everything up to this point has been prep. This step is about movement. If they don't feel progress in the first few days, they won't feel it later.

Trigger action that feels achievable

Design the first milestone or task to deliver a result – not just a checkbox. Keep it short enough to complete quickly, meaningful enough to matter, and clearly linked to the transformation they signed up for.

This might be identifying a key constraint, completing a diagnostic, setting a 30-day focus, or completing their first decision-making template.

The outcome isn't mastery – it's movement.

Reinforce progress with visibility

Once someone acts, amplify it. That might be through coach feedback, community recognition, visible tracking, or milestone shoutouts. When progress is seen, it multiplies.

When learners see themselves moving – and see others moving alongside them – the experience becomes magnetic.

The goal here isn't volume. It's belief. Belief that this works. Belief that they're capable. Belief that they're already further than they were yesterday.

Lock it in before you launch

Before you open the doors, your access experience needs to be more than functional – it needs to build belief, set the tone, and generate immediate motion.

To complete this stage:

- Craft a welcome that leads with clarity and energy.
- Build a first-72-hour journey that turns attention into traction.
- Communicate the program's rhythm early and often.
- Create a fast, meaningful win to spark belief.

When learners feel confident, clear, and in motion from the beginning, you don't just welcome them. You activate them.

That's the power of intentional access. And it's the foundation of a journey they'll want to stay in.

WHAT'S NEXT?

Your offer is no longer a loose idea.
It's structured. It's sequenced. It's ready
to serve.

Now we focus on **sustaining it, scaling
it, and sharing it** – with the right tools,
positioning, metrics, and feedback systems
to help your hybrid program grow without
burning you out.

Part VII

SUSTAINING AND SHARING YOUR HYBRID EXPERIENCE

"

Blended learning allows us to create more dynamic and engaging learning experiences for students.

Tony Wagner[10]

"

---

10 Tony Wagner is a globally recognized expert in education, known for his work on transforming education to meet the needs of the 21st century.

Now that your hybrid experience is built, how do you **get it into the hands of the right people**?

This part covers marketing, positioning, and outreach with clarity and confidence. You'll also learn how to track the right metrics and keep your offer alive, relevant, and growing.

This is your **go-to-market strategy** – hybrid-style.

21

Tech that works for you, not against you

You've already done the hard part – designing a powerful, transformation-focused program using the Hybrid Authority Formula. You've clarified your content, built the bones of a real community, embedded collaborative practice, and created space for coaching that drives meaningful momentum. Now, the real question is: how do you deliver that experience again and again, without bottlenecking your capacity, compromising the transformation, or relying on systems that fall apart under pressure?

This chapter isn't about finding the perfect software. It's about defining the functional architecture that upholds your hybrid delivery model. It's about choosing delivery infrastructure that scales with you – not tech for tech's sake, but systems that sustain the promise of transformation.

Technology should serve the experience not shape it

If you're not intentional, your tech stack starts leading the design instead of supporting it. The more disconnected platforms you add, the harder it becomes to maintain a coherent experience. You've already designed the journey. Your delivery systems should simply enable that journey to be lived consistently by every learner, no matter how many people you serve.

This means your technology needs to disappear into the background. Not because it's invisible, but because it's intuitive. Seamless. Aligned. When a learner enters your world, they shouldn't be met with a maze of logins and links – they should be met with flow. They should feel like the entire system is designed with their success in mind. Because it is.

Every decision about your tools should come down to: does this make the Hybrid Authority Formula easier to deliver, easier to sustain, and easier to elevate? If the answer is no, it doesn't belong.

Delivering the four pillars requires system support

Each pillar of the Hybrid Authority Formula demands its own delivery structure. You've already mapped what transformation looks like – now you need systems that let that transformation happen without reinventing the wheel.

Your content delivery system should be rock solid. This is where your digital twin lives – not just videos on a page, but an experience that unfolds with clarity and precision. Your platform must enable pacing, access, reflection, and next-step logic. When done well, the learner always knows where they are and what's next, without you needing to manually direct them.

Your community environment must be consistent, curated, and culturally aligned to the transformation. The platform itself is just the shell – what matters is the cadence of interaction, the visibility of leadership, and the mechanisms for accountability. This isn't a 'group chat' – it's a relational container with intention. The right infrastructure creates rhythm and ownership, so you're not carrying the emotional weight of keeping everyone connected.

Collaboration comes to life through structure. Whether that's shared challenges, feedback loops, peer-to-peer implementation formats, or cohort-based sprints, the platform must support shared progress. Your tech should reduce ambiguity, provide visibility, and allow learners to engage with each other's work in a way that deepens learning, not distracts from it.

Coaching requires clarity. If it's one-on-one, there must be boundaries, booking systems, and pre-qualification to protect your energy and maximize your impact. If it's group-based, your system must support facilitation structure, follow-up, and integration. Coaching cannot be a free-for-all inbox. It must be defined, contained, and supported.

Complexity is not a badge of honor

Many experts assume that scaling means building a sophisticated tech ecosystem. But complexity is not a sign of professionalism – it's a sign of a lack of focus. The most scalable delivery systems are usually the simplest. They do exactly what they need to do, nothing more.

Simplicity protects your attention. It reduces learner friction. And it makes it easier to maintain consistency, especially when you bring in team members, partners, or facilitators to help deliver the experience. You shouldn't be the only person who knows how it works. A simple, well-documented delivery system is a leadership asset, not just an operational one.

Integration creates trust

The learner experience isn't defined by the number of tools – it's defined by how the tools work together. Every time a learner must jump from one place to another, they lose a little momentum. Every time they aren't sure what's next, they feel resistance.

Smooth transitions build confidence. They let your learners stay focused on the work, not on navigating the back end. The more integrated your delivery infrastructure, the more seamless the journey feels. And the more seamless it feels, the more powerful the transformation becomes.

You're not automating to escape, you're designing to show up where it matters

Operational delivery is not about removing yourself. It's about removing the *repetitive tasks that dilute your presence.*

When your systems carry the baseline functions, you can show up with energy, clarity, and focus in the moments that require your voice, your guidance, your insight. That's where your impact is felt most.

You're not vanishing. You're architecting. You're building the infrastructure that allows your program to breathe – even when your calendar is full, your team expands, or your audience scales.

That's the difference between a tech stack and a delivery system. One adds tools. The other delivers transformation.

This is how you make the Hybrid Authority Formula real – every time, for every learner, without compromising the quality you built it on.

22

Positioning your program with authority

Designing a transformative program is one thing. Getting the right people to engage with it is something else entirely. And yet, far too many brilliant programs sit untouched – not because the offer lacks power, but because the marketing lacks clarity, resonance, or integrity.

Marketing a hybrid program is not about hype, hustle, or hacks. It's about crafting a message that reflects the depth of your work and reaching the people who genuinely need what you've built. When done well, marketing doesn't feel like selling. It feels like inviting the right learners into a story they want to be part of.

It starts with them

Every effective marketing campaign begins not with a funnel, but with empathy. You can't enrol someone in a learning journey until you understand the journey they're already on. That means stepping into their world. What are they struggling with? What keeps them stuck? What language do they use to describe their problems? What outcomes are they hungry for?

Empathy mapping isn't fluff – it's strategy. When you understand what your learners think, feel, say, and do in relation to their goals, you can build a bridge between where they are and what you offer. Surveys, interviews, and open conversations become tools of clarity. They aren't just ways to validate an idea – they're how you learn to speak in your audience's language instead of your own.

This isn't market research as a tick-box exercise. This is you, as the creator, taking responsibility for truly understanding the transformation you're promising from the perspective of those experiencing the problem. That level of empathy creates messaging that cuts through.

Story first, format second

The Hybrid Authority Formula is powerful, but the fact that it blends content, community, collaboration, and coaching is not the hook. The real story is the transformation. The shift. The outcome that matters.

When you communicate your program, you're not selling modules, templates, or group calls. You're selling a better version of the future. A more confident voice. A clearer strategy. A business that no longer relies on burnout. That's what lands. That's what opens doors. That's what invites trust.

Your marketing must move beyond features and tap into emotion, identity, and meaning. That doesn't mean being manipulative – it means being human. Use story. Show the journey. Let your marketing reflect the values of your program. And don't be afraid to share why you built this experience. Your reasons are often more compelling than your roadmap.

Social media is the amplifier

If content is the message, social media is the amplifier. But it's not about being everywhere or dancing on reels. It's about choosing channels where your audience already lives and then showing up with consistency and value.

Every post is a chance to teach something, challenge something, or show something real. It's not about broadcasting. It's about beginning conversations. The more you engage – not perform – the more your authority grows. Social media done well isn't a stage. It's a table. You're not lecturing. You're inviting.

Use it to let people experience your teaching. Give value upfront. Build relationships. Then, when the time is right to invite them into your program, they're already halfway bought in – not because of a sales tactic, but because of trust.

Content marketing that positions you as the authority

Your content is more than promotion – it's proof. When you publish articles, share frameworks, or host value-driven webinars, you're not just building visibility. You're building confidence. Content that teaches is content that converts – because it demonstrates your expertise without having to claim it.

Create materials that solve the small problems in your audience's world and they'll trust you to help solve the big ones. And don't underestimate the power of consistency. One great post is helpful. A steady stream of insight is what builds your brand.

Simple beats clever. Clear beats cute. Your marketing messages need to feel like they were pulled from your audience's journal, not a copywriting handbook. When someone reads your words, they should feel seen – not sold to.

The best messages don't list features. They paint possibility. They speak to pain and progress. They make the transformation feel real before the purchase ever happens.

This is where great marketing earns its weight. It doesn't just get people to click. It gets them to believe. And belief is the path to enrolment.

Integrity, not hype

You don't need to exaggerate your outcomes when your learners can speak for themselves. Testimonials, case studies, and success stories are some of your most valuable assets – not because they sell, but because they show. Real stories, real people, real progress.

Highlight the wins. Share the process. Show the before-and-after. Let your learners become your advocates – not because you asked them to, but because your program earned it.

Success stories create social proof without sounding promotional. When framed with integrity, they become signals of transformation, not trophies.

It's tempting to follow trends. To write louder headlines. To push urgency and scarcity to unnatural levels. But the cost is credibility. You built your hybrid program to offer real transformation. Your marketing should reflect that.

Avoid gimmicks. Lead with truth. Stay human. Build a system that respects your audience's intelligence. That's how you attract learners who are aligned – not just buyers who are reactive.

You are not just selling a program. You're stewarding a promise. Market accordingly.

The invitation is part of the experience

Marketing isn't a separate activity. It's the first step of the journey. When done well, it creates clarity, builds desire, and welcomes the right people into your world. That's not hype. That's leadership.

So tell the story. Share the why. Show the transformation. And invite people in – not to buy something, but to become something.

That's how you market a Hybrid Authority experience. And that's how you become known for the change you create, not the content you deliver.

23

The metrics that matter

You cannot improve what you do not measure. And you cannot measure what you have not clearly defined. That's the simple truth behind program success. Whether you're delivering a one-week masterclass, a six-month certification, or a long-term coaching ecosystem, the moment you start treating your learning experience like a serious product, you need serious measurement.

Measuring success is not about chasing dashboard vanity. It's about choosing metrics that reflect the outcomes you promised, the experience you designed, and the transformations your learners expect. Metrics are how you check your alignment. They tell you if your intentions are translating into results.

So what do you measure? How do you know what matters? And how do you stop drowning in data that looks impressive but offers no insight?

First define what success looks like

Success must be defined in advance. Before you decide on metrics, you need to decide what a successful learner journey looks like. Not what feels good to report. Not what sounds impressive on social media. But what tells you, unambiguously, that learning is happening, momentum is building, and transformation is taking root.

Start with outcomes. What do learners walk away with? What change are they meant to experience? Is it a skill? A mindset shift? A tangible result in their business or life? From there, define what evidence of that change looks like. That's the foundation for meaningful metrics.

Build a performance dashboard you actually use

Once you've defined your success outcomes, you can build a dashboard that works. That dashboard should give you three types of information:

- **First, track learner activity.** You need to know how people are engaging. Are they showing up? Are they moving through your content or assignments? Where do they drop off? This gives you operational insight.

- **Second, capture progress indicators.** What milestones are being reached? Are people applying what they learn? Are they submitting work? Reporting outcomes? Booking calls? This tells you if learning is translating into action.

- **Third, collect qualitative feedback.** This is the nuance. What are learners saying about their experience? What do they feel? What do they wish had been different?

What are they doing differently in their real lives or work? This gives you developmental insight.

The goal isn't just to collect metrics. It's to *use* them. You need a snapshot that shows you what's working, what's drifting, and what needs to be addressed – ideally, every week during delivery, and in every post-program review.

Choose metrics that reveal patterns, not just data points

It's tempting to track everything, but most metrics are noise unless they reveal something you can act on. If a stat goes up or down and you don't know what to do about it, it's not worth tracking.

Here's what really matters:

- Completion rates only matter if they correlate with outcomes. Someone finishing doesn't mean they transformed. But when high completion aligns with strong learner outcomes, it tells you your structure is working.

- Session duration can indicate interest and pacing. If people drop off early or skip sections, it may signal content overload or misalignment. If they stay engaged longer than expected, that's a sign of emotional investment or flow.

- Application metrics are where the gold lies. If your program includes implementation exercises, submissions, or real-world action, track them. This shows you whether your content is activating change or just informing.

- Feedback scores offer a pulse on satisfaction. But dig deeper. Don't just ask, 'Did you enjoy it?' Ask what surprised them, what they'll take forward, and what almost made them quit. The goal is insight, not affirmation.

- Live session attendance tells you how important your synchronous touchpoints are. But if attendance drops, that doesn't automatically mean disengagement – it could mean your asynchronous experience is strong enough to stand alone. Interpret context, not just numbers.

- Referral or re-enrolment rates may be your clearest indicators of value. If people are telling others or returning for more, you're doing something worth scaling.

Build a feedback loop that drives action

Feedback isn't a favor. It's a performance tool – and like any tool, it needs to be designed, sharpened, and used deliberately. Passive feedback collection – hoping someone fills in a survey or leaves a nice comment – is not enough. You need intentional checkpoints that invite learner insight at specific points in their journey:

- After onboarding, ask about clarity. Did they understand how the program worked? Were expectations clear?
- Midway through the program, check on momentum. Are they still engaged? Do they feel supported?
- At the end, get insight into transformation. What changed? What would they have changed about the program?

But asking for feedback isn't enough. You need to interpret it. Go beyond what was said and look for what it means. If a learner calls a module 'overwhelming,' is it a content problem? A pacing issue? A support gap? Feedback rarely hands you the answer – it signals where to look. That's your role as a program operator: to read between the lines, ask the follow-up questions, and connect feedback to behavior patterns in your data.

And most importantly, close the loop. Show your learners that you listened. When changes are made, name them. When feedback reveals a trend, explain how it will shape the next iteration. This isn't just about improvement – it's about building trust. Learners who feel heard stay longer, engage deeper, and refer more often. Feedback is not the end of a conversation. It's the beginning of better delivery.

Make metrics part of your leadership practice

As the creator, you're not just the teacher – you're the strategist. Data allows you to lead with clarity. It allows you to make decisions with confidence. It allows you to improve with intention.

When you take your metrics seriously, you take your learners seriously. You show them that their progress matters – and that every part of your program is designed with their success in mind. This is not just something you're passionate about; it's a structured, professional commitment to delivering results that matter in the real world.

So build your dashboard. Define what success looks like. Track what matters. And act on what you learn.

That's not just measurement. That's leadership. And that's how your program doesn't just get built – it gets better every single time.

24

Evolve with your learners

The most dangerous myth in learning design is that the hard work is done once the program is built. That the magic lives in the curriculum, the slides, or the videos. But transformation doesn't come from content – it comes from what happens *after* the launch. Real learning programs aren't static. They're living systems. And like any living thing, they either adapt or decay.

A program's relevance isn't defined by how good it was when you released it. It's defined by how well it stays aligned to what your learners need next. That means being in a constant state of observation, refinement, and readiness to evolve. Not reactively, and not just when numbers start dipping, but proactively, by embedding the principle of continuous improvement into how your program is run.

What continuous improvement really looks like

Continuous improvement doesn't mean rewriting everything every few months or chasing the latest trend. It means putting systems in place to help you regularly spot what's working, where friction is building, and how learner expectations are shifting. It's a disciplined rhythm of checking, learning, and improving.

You need structured reflection points – after each module, at the end of every cohort, and periodically across your delivery cycles. You need to actively collect and analyze qualitative feedback and engagement data. And you need the courage to act on what you find.

Improvement isn't always dramatic. Sometimes, it's as simple as rewording an instruction that's causing confusion, adding a new resource to bridge a learning gap, or restructuring the pacing so momentum builds instead of fizzling. It's the accumulated value of small refinements that creates big impact.

When you listen, you lead

The most valuable insights often come from the learners who challenge your assumptions. The participant who didn't finish the course. The one who paused halfway through. The one who questioned a model you've used for years. Their feedback isn't a threat – it's a mirror. It reflects where your program might be falling short – not in theory, but in practice.

This is why proximity matters. You can't lead from a distance. You need to stay close enough to your learners to hear the nuances in their language, to observe where energy levels drop, and to pick up patterns that raw metrics miss. When you listen deeply, you don't just solve problems – you anticipate them.

That doesn't mean you take every piece of feedback at face value. It means you learn to look for trends. You study the gaps between what you intended and how it landed. You build the habit of asking: is this still working? Is this still necessary? Is this still true?

Evolving content, delivery, and support

Your content will age. Even evergreen ideas become less effective as the world changes around them. The examples that resonated last year might feel irrelevant now. The case studies you used when you started might be missing the depth or diversity today's learners expect.

Evolution doesn't mean starting over. It means iterating, one layer at a time. It might mean refining your onboarding flow so learners feel momentum from day one. It might mean reorganizing modules for better cognitive load. Or reworking your support structure so help feels accessible before it's desperately needed.

Even your coaching structures, facilitation methods, and community rhythms need periodic review. Are they delivering what they used to? Are they still aligned with your vision for transformation? Have you, as the leader, outgrown your own program?

Building evolution into your culture

Programs that improve are programs that are built to improve. That means moving from ad hoc reflection to embedded review. Establish quarterly retrospectives. Collect structured learner feedback, not just testimonials. Make data review a standing item in your operations. This isn't about being hyper-optimized. It's about becoming resilient.

Improvement shouldn't happen only when something breaks. It should happen because growth is built into the DNA of your delivery. A culture of evolution is what prevents irrelevance. It's what keeps your learning alive. And it's what makes learners come back – not just for more content, but because they trust that your program doesn't stand still.

Continuous improvement is strategic, not cosmetic

The risk with continuous improvement is that it becomes cosmetic: tweaks that feel productive but don't change outcomes. A new template. A slicker visual. A renamed module. That's not evolution – it's distraction.

Improvement that matters starts with learner outcomes. Are they getting further? Are they getting there faster? Are they getting stuck in the same places? Are they applying what they learn in the real world? That's the data that matters. That's where change begins.

This is not about perfection. It's about momentum. Your program doesn't need to be flawless – it needs to be adaptive. When you build to improve, you protect your authority. You earn trust. You ensure that the promise you made at launch is still being delivered, years later.

This is the work of a learning leader – not just someone who builds a great program once, but someone who makes that program better every time it runs. That's what your learners deserve. And that's how you stay relevant – not just now, but for the long run.

25

How to expand without exploding

You've built something powerful. You've created an experience that transforms. And now, your next move isn't about doing more – it's about doing it differently. This chapter isn't about bigger launches or heavier delivery. It's about how to take the transformation you've created and scale it beyond yourself, without diluting the depth, losing control, or burning out.

Your next move

Growth doesn't have to mean complexity. Expansion doesn't have to mean exhaustion. The most sustainable and strategic next moves are ones that multiply your impact, not your workload.

Let's explore what that can look like.

Licensing: scaling without delivery

When you've developed a proven methodology, there comes a point where delivering it yourself becomes the bottleneck. Licensing gives you a way to scale your intellectual property without having to scale your time.

By packaging your program and licensing it to other professionals – whether facilitators, consultants, internal L&D teams, or partner organizations – you create a model where others deliver your content, under your brand, with your standards.

This move isn't just about revenue. It's about reach. It allows you to take a model that works and let it live in new markets, new contexts, and new communities, without you having to be there.

To do this well, you need clarity around your frameworks, delivery structure, assets, and quality control. You're not just handing someone your slides – you're inviting them to uphold your methodology. That means training, certification, or at the very least, clear guidelines that protect the learner experience.

Certification: turning your learners into leaders

Some learners don't just want to apply your work – they want to embody it. Certification lets them do that. By building a certification pathway, you invite your best learners to deepen their commitment, develop mastery, and become advocates for your methodology.

Certification adds structure and accountability to what might otherwise be informal knowledge transfer. It allows you to build a network of aligned professionals who share your values, language, and delivery principles.

When designed well, certification becomes more than a badge. It becomes a community. A source of referrals. A pipeline for future collaborators or delivery partners. And a multiplier of your reputation.

Team delivery: letting go without letting down

If your program is already running with consistency and you're reaching capacity, the next move might not be to grow the audience – it might be to grow the team.

Hiring facilitators, coaches, or delivery support allows you to maintain program integrity while removing yourself from the frontline. But this only works if your program is systemised. You need clear SOPs, training assets, escalation protocols, and coaching guidelines. You're not duplicating your presence – you're scaling the process.

This shift does more than reduce your calendar load. It sends a powerful message to your learners: this is not a one-person show. It's a professional ecosystem. A structured experience that doesn't rely on individual genius, but on collective delivery excellence.

Strategic partnerships: borrowing authority and expanding access

Sometimes, the fastest way to grow is to align with someone who already has the audience, infrastructure, or influence you need. Strategic partnerships – whether with associations, enterprise clients, or aligned creators – can open doors that individual marketing cannot.

These partnerships can take many forms: co-branded delivery, white-labeled versions of your program, bundled offers, or internal team training. The key is to maintain clarity about your non-negotiables.

Not all growth is good growth. If a partner dilutes your brand, breaks your methodology, or compromises learner experience, the cost is too high.

But when aligned well, partnerships are leverage. They give you reach without reinventing your offer.

Stepping into the architect role

Whatever your next move is, the shift is the same: you're not the expert at the center anymore. You're the architect above it. Your job isn't to deliver every result – it's to design the infrastructure, relationships, and systems that allow others to deliver it with you, or without you.

This shift isn't just logistical. It's identity-level. You go from teacher to leader. From provider to platform. From presence-driven to process-driven. And that's what turns a great program into a movement.

The best next move isn't always more. Sometimes it's less, but smarter. Sometimes it's letting go so others can carry it further. And sometimes, it's stepping back just enough to see the bigger game you're here to play.

Whatever you choose, let it be intentional. Let it be strategic. And let it be in service of the impact you set out to create.

You're not done. You're just getting started.

26

Staying human in the age of AI

As we close out this book, it's important to zoom out and consider where the learning industry is heading. Not in the next decade, but in the next 12 months. Because the exploding pace of change isn't theoretical anymore. It's real. And it's being driven by technology, especially artificial intelligence.

This matters because if you've followed the Hybrid Authority Formula so far, you know that the model is built on an intentional blend of digital content and human experience. That blend is more critical now than ever before. Why? Because the digital side of learning is being rapidly accelerated by automation and AI. What used to be a differentiator – clean modules, strong frameworks, even solid instructional design – is becoming replicable by machines.

But here's the truth: transformation isn't just about access to content. It's about guidance, support, challenge, and care. AI can replicate delivery. It cannot replicate depth. Your competitive edge won't come from avoiding tech – it'll come from integrating it. The future isn't human *or* machine. It's a sophisticated blend of both. That's the heart of hybrid – and it's why we need to talk about AI now.

Let's drop the polite preamble. The learning industry is being rewritten – right now. Not next year. Not when the tools are more mature. Now.

AI is no longer emerging. It's embedded. And if your learning program isn't evolving with it, you're already playing catch-up. This isn't fearmongering. It's fact. What used to differentiate your offer – your knowledge, your frameworks, your structure – is rapidly becoming replicable. What once took you weeks to design, an AI can draft in minutes. And what once made you stand out – your voice, your clarity, your instructional design – can now be mimicked with shocking precision.

So, what does that mean for you?

It means you either adapt – intelligently and intentionally – or you risk irrelevance.

But here's the good news: you're not competing *with* AI. You're competing *without* it. And that's a battle you don't want to fight.

This is not about hype – it's about adaptation

Artificial intelligence isn't going to replace transformational education. But it will absolutely replace anyone who refuses to evolve how they design, deliver, and support that education.

You are no longer just an expert. You are a system builder. A transformation designer. A community architect. And now, like it or not, you are a curator of the human-technology interface. That role demands new awareness, new thinking, and new tools.

Your learners won't stop needing guidance, support, or accountability. But they will expect faster answers, more personalized journeys, and richer learning experiences. AI isn't just shaping their expectations – it's shaping their standards.

Let AI do the work it's built for

Begin with your bottlenecks. That clunky onboarding email series. The weekly follow-up reminders. The post-coaching call notes. The lesson outline that takes two hours to sketch. The quiz you've been meaning to create for six months.

AI doesn't replace the insight. It replaces the inefficiency.

You still bring the transformation. The nuance. The discernment. But you no longer need to build every piece by hand. Use AI tools to:

- draft initial content and refine it with your voice
- summarize and organize learner submissions
- generate follow-up tasks, reflective questions, or personalized resources based on learner activity
- create structured assessments or knowledge checks in minutes.

This isn't about reducing quality. It's about removing friction. You're not outsourcing your authority. You're streamlining the admin that drains it.

Use AI to elevate, not imitate

This is the frontier where Bloom's 2 Sigma Problem becomes relevant. In the 1980s, educational psychologist Benjamin Bloom showed that students receiving one-on-one tutoring performed two standard deviations better than those in traditional classrooms. The challenge, known as the '2 Sigma Problem,' was how to replicate the results of personal tutoring at scale. For decades, the answer was: you can't – unless you have endless resources. But today, AI may finally provide a pathway.

We're already seeing this in action. Georgia Tech's use of an AI teaching assistant, dubbed 'Jill Watson,' revolutionised how they handled student support at scale – responding to thousands of queries with speed and precision, freeing up human educators to focus on deeper, more strategic teaching. Or take Duolingo's chatbots, which allow learners to practise conversations in real time, without fear of judgment or embarrassment. That's not just AI being clever. That's AI enhancing safety, access, and application.

Then there's Carnegie Learning, a platform that personalizes math instruction using adaptive algorithms. It reads patterns in student responses and dynamically adjusts instructions in real time – offering instant feedback tailored to where a learner is stuck or succeeding. These aren't science fiction case studies. They're proof points. And they're a reminder that AI can do more than just automate – it can elevate the learning experience when applied with intention.

If your program simply becomes faster or prettier because of AI, you've missed the point. The real power is in enhancing the learner experience. And that starts with looking at how AI can help you *respond* better to learner needs.

Imagine having instant insight into which modules learners are struggling with – before they tell you. Or being able to generate personalized learning suggestions based on their progress and questions. Or delivering tailored nudges at just the right moment to keep someone engaged when motivation dips. Better yet, imagine integrating a personalized AI coach into your program – one that operates as a scalable version of your guidance, offering on-demand micro-coaching, nudges, reflections, and contextual prompts based on real-time learner data. It doesn't replace your coaching – it amplifies it, by being present in the moments you physically can't be. That's how you deliver the feel of one-to-one support without carrying the full weight yourself.

That's what intelligent education looks like. And it's possible now – not in the future. You just have to stop designing programs like it's 2019.

Future-proofing your authority means embracing change

The fastest way to become obsolete is to stay static. If your value is rooted only in what you know, you're replaceable. If your value is rooted in how you guide, adapt, facilitate, and build transformation at scale, you're irreplaceable.

This chapter isn't here to tell you which tools to use. That changes monthly. It's here to shift your posture from protective to progressive. The educators who will thrive are those who experiment early, fail fast, learn rapidly, and retain what works. Not the ones who wait for permission or perfection.

So, what does that look like?

You build an AI-enabled onboarding journey that adjusts pacing and content based on initial learner responses. You use AI-powered feedback assistants that suggest personalized next steps based on submitted work. You analyze behavioral data to improve module sequencing. You pre-fill lesson outlines and design assets so you can spend more time improving outcomes and less time formatting slides.

And most of all, you stop seeing AI as a threat to your brand and start seeing it as a tool that strengthens your delivery.

The human layer is still the most valuable

AI can speed up production. It can mimic tone. It can even run conversations. But it cannot earn trust. It cannot lead with presence. It cannot offer grounded judgment, lived experience, or emotionally attuned support. And it can't create communities that hold people through uncertainty, doubt, or transformation.

That's your role. That's the role that remains untouched – and in fact, becomes *more valuable* as the noise increases.

In the age of AI, humanity is the premium layer. So double down on what only you can do. Bring your stories. Your facilitation. Your clarity. And then use AI to support and scale it – not replace it.

This is not optional – it's strategic

AI will change how programs are built, marketed, delivered, and experienced. That's inevitable. The question is: will you shape that change, or be shaped by it?

You don't need to know everything. But you do need to begin. Start small. Start somewhere. Start today.

Learn just enough to ask better questions. Play with tools. Set constraints. Run tests. And make AI integration a standing part of your development and delivery conversations.

The future of learning is not either/or. It's both. Tech and touch. Speed and substance. Intelligence and intuition.

If you want to lead the next era of learning, you can't just be a great educator. You must be an adaptive one.

And if you've made it this far through this book, that's already who you are.

Now go prove it.

WHAT'S NEXT?

The offer is built. The delivery is working. The systems are in place.

But there's one more shift ahead – the one that changes everything.

In this final part, we move from building the experience to **owning the identity**. This is where you fully step into your authority, lead from your values, and expand your work into its next evolution.

Part VIII

FROM AUTHORITY TO ACTION

"

Learning is not the product of teaching. Learning is the product of the activity of learners.

John Holt[11]

"

---

11 John Holt was an American educator and author best known for his criticism of
traditional schooling and his advocacy for self-directed learning.

You're not just an expert anymore. You're the architect of transformation.

In this final part, we zoom out. You've built a hybrid model, clarified your IP, and crafted a delivery system that scales. Now it's time to own the identity shift – from coach to category leader.

You'll explore your evolution as an authority, how to expand your reach, and what it means to **lead learning in the age of AI and automation**.

27

From expert to authority

Owning the identity shift

There comes a point in every expert's journey where strategy alone is no longer the answer. You've built the program, defined the transformation, mapped the learner journey. And yet – something internal hasn't quite caught up. That 'something' is identity.

This chapter is about closing that gap.

Because while the Hybrid Authority Formula gives you the structure to scale, what ultimately sustains it is how you see yourself. If you still carry the mindset of a freelancer, a technician, or a service provider – even with a brilliant program behind you – you'll keep operating from that place. You'll hesitate. You'll defer. You'll play small. The real shift isn't just building the system. It's owning your role as the person who leads it.

Let's name the progression: you began as a knowledge holder. Someone who had answers, frameworks, and experience that could help others. Then, you became a learning designer – someone who intentionally crafts experiences that create change. And now, you're being asked to step into the role of authority architect. Not just delivering information, but building the systems, structures, and standards that shape how others grow.

That shift is psychological. Emotional. And for many, uncomfortable.

Because stepping into authority means facing down the voice that says, 'You're not ready.' It means noticing the hesitation that surfaces when you're about to price higher, be more visible, or take up more space. It means acknowledging the pull to keep overdelivering instead of trusting your system. These are not weaknesses. They're signs that you're evolving.

Imposter syndrome doesn't go away by working harder. It quiets when you start honoring the evidence. The results you've created. The value you've built. The integrity you've shown. The way your learners speak about the impact you've made. That's the proof. And it's time you believed it.

Authority isn't claimed in a tagline or on a sales page. It's built on the quiet consistency of delivering transformation, again and again. It's forged in the moments where you choose clarity over chaos, structure over scrambling, and leadership over labor.

You're not just the face of your program. You're the architect of its impact.

That means designing with precision. Showing up with intention. And leading with a mindset that says: I've done the work. I know what I'm building. And I'm ready to stand behind it.

Most people never make this shift

Most people will never make this shift. They'll keep chasing the next tactic. They'll keep doing everything manually. They'll keep defining their value by the hours they work or the number of clients they serve. But you're not most people. You're someone who's chosen to lead with design, deliver with depth, and scale without compromise.

And yes – there will be moments of doubt. But doubt is not disqualification. It's an invitation to step up. To trust the structure you've built. To believe in the transformation you've mapped. And to move forward as the authority you've already become.

This isn't about becoming someone new. It's about finally recognizing who you've already grown into.

That's the real shift. And it's yours to own.

28

Make it real

Your action plan and next steps

This is the part where most people stop.

They read the book. They highlight the good bits. They tell themselves, 'That's exactly what I need to do.' And then they move on to the next big idea, and stay exactly where they are.

But not you.

You're still here because you're ready to move. Not just think differently. Not just plan better. But *do*. And that's what this final chapter is about: translating everything you've learned into tangible next steps that move your Hybrid Authority Formula out of your head and into the world.

You don't need another course. You don't need a certification. You don't need perfect conditions. You need clarity, commitment, and momentum. Here's how you create it.

If you haven't started yet: begin with the core

Strip away the noise and start with the most important question: what is the transformation you're offering? Not what content you want to deliver. Not what features you want to include. But what change are you here to create? That's your anchor.

Once you've defined the transformation, design backward. What does the learner need to know, believe, and do to get there? What structure, support, and environment will help them do it? That's your Hybrid Blueprint.

Choose one person to design it for. Not your market – your learner. Think of someone real. Someone whose life would change because of this experience. Build it for them. You can scale later. Right now, you need resonance.

Then, sketch the four pillars:

- What content will they need to absorb on their own?
- Where will they connect with others?
- How will they apply what they learn, with support?
- Where will your guidance show up, and how?

Your first version doesn't need to be automated, branded, or even paid. But it does need to be structured. Structure creates confidence – for them, and for you.

If you've already built something: audit and refine

If you've already launched a program, it's time to revisit it through the Hybrid Authority lens.

Ask yourself:

- Does my content act like a true digital twin – or am I still manually explaining everything?
- Is my community intentional and guided – or just a passive forum?

- Are learners collaborating – or just consuming?
- Is coaching showing up in the right places – or is it spread thin across everything?

Wherever the gaps are, don't panic. You don't need to rebuild. You need to refine. Start with the pillar that feels weakest and strengthen its structure.

Then look at your delivery. Are your systems supporting scale, or suffocating you? Is your tech stack amplifying your model, or creating confusion? Is your data giving you insight, or just numbers?

Audit. Simplify. Improve. That's how great programs evolve.

Set a 90-day plan

Vision is long-term. Authority is built one decision at a time.

So what will you do in the next 90 days to bring this work to life?

- Will you launch a beta version of your program?
- Will you test a group coaching model?
- Will you rebuild your curriculum around the four pillars?
- Will you replace your manual onboarding with a guided digital journey?
- Will you run your first pilot, even if it's imperfect?

Pick one commitment for each pillar. Then build your delivery rhythm around it. Not just what you'll build, but *when* you'll deliver, review, and refine.

This isn't about speed. It's about motion. Start small. But start.

Step into the role you've designed for yourself

Everything you need is already here. The tools. The insight. The framework. The philosophy.

What happens next is up to you.

You don't need permission. You need practice.

You don't need more time. You need better boundaries.

You don't need to master everything. You need to lead something.

This is how movements begin – not with a bang, but with a decision.

You've built the map.

Now take the next step.

You're not just running a program. You're raising a standard.

And the world is watching. So, let's go.

If you need help

You've made it to the end of the book – but in many ways, this is where the real work begins. Designing a transformational learning experience is one thing. Delivering it, scaling it, and living into the authority you've built? That's an entirely different level of leadership.

The Hybrid Authority Formula is now yours to work with. You've got the structure. The mindset. The clarity. But if you'd like help making it real – support with building, launching, or refining your program – we're here to help.

The Ultimate Leverage Blueprint is our implementation-focused program where we walk you through building your hybrid program, step by step. You'll go beyond theory and into execution. From offer design and learner journey mapping, to content creation, delivery systems, marketing, and launch support, we don't just help you think it through. We help you *build it out.*

You'll be surrounded by a community of experts like you – coaches, consultants, educators, and facilitators – who are committed to delivering deep transformation without burning out or staying stuck in one-on-one delivery. Inside the program, you'll get access to templates, reviews, live support, and real feedback – not fluff, not theory, and not more stuff to file. Just momentum.

This is the environment where your ideas become assets. Where your curriculum becomes a system. And where your work starts reaching the people who need it most.

If that sounds like the next step for you, visit:

leverageyourexpertise.online/1offer

If you've got a question, a challenge, or just want to reach out directly, email us at:

hello@mavenzeal.com.au

You're building something meaningful, don't do it alone.

We'd be honored to support you in making your Hybrid Authority vision a reality.

Because this is more than a model. It's a movement.

And you're ready to lead it.

About the author

Matthew Mason is a learning strategist, systems thinker, and the founder of Mavenzeal – a digital learning consultancy that partners with coaches, consultants, and expert educators to turn their intellectual property into powerful, scalable programs. Known for blending instructional design excellence with real-world business acumen, Matthew helps his clients build education ecosystems that are impactful, sustainable, and designed for scale.

His path into the learning world was anything but linear. Originally working as a trainer in the racing industry, Matthew pivoted into adult education after discovering a gift for teaching people – first in the field, then across sectors. His passion for helping others learn evolved into a pursuit of learning design mastery, which led him to work with organisations ranging from government agencies to multinational companies, universities, and fast-moving expert-led businesses across Australia and Southeast Asia.

When the COVID-19 pandemic disrupted the way education was delivered, Matthew was already ahead of the curve. He began working closely with independent experts to codify and digitise their IP – helping them move beyond overbooked calendars and into programs that delivered depth, results, and reach. His frameworks focus not just on what to teach, but on how to architect real transformation.

Matthew is a multi-award-winning learning designer and strategist, recognized as the **Learning and Development Professional of the Year** by the Australian Learning Impact Awards. He is a Certified Learning Professional (CLP) and a Certified Online Learning Facilitator (COLF), respected for helping subject matter experts evolve into education leaders.

Through his signature frameworks – including the Hybrid Authority Formula and the Ultimate Leverage Blueprint – Matthew empowers experts to shift from knowledge holders to transformational authorities. He is a sought-after speaker, facilitator, and thought leader, having delivered keynotes and workshops across Australia, the United Kingdom, and Singapore.

Matthew's mission is simple: to help experts design learning that not only informs – but transforms. And to ensure that the leaders shaping the future of education are doing it with structure, integrity, and serious impact.